How to Measure Performance and Use Tests

Lynn Lyons Morris
Carol Taylor Fitz-Gibbon
Elaine Lindheim

Center for the Study of Evaluation
University of California, Los Angeles

SAGE Publications
International Educational and Professional Publisher
Newbury Park London New Delhi

The second edition of the *Program Evaluation Kit* was developed at the Center for the Study of Evaluation, Graduate School of Education, University of California.

The development of this second edition of the CSE *Program Evaluation Kit* was supported in part by a grant from the National Institute of Education, currently known as the Office of Educational Research and Improvement. However, the opinions expressed herein do not necessarily reflect the position or policy of that agency and no official endorsement should be inferred.

The second edition of the *Program Evaluation Kit* is published and distributed by Sage Publications, Inc, Newbury Park, California, under an exclusive agreement with The Regents of the University of California.

For information address:

SAGE Publications, Inc.
2455 Teller Road
Newbury Park, California 91320
E-mail: order@sagepub.com

SAGE Publications Ltd.
6 Bonhill Street
London EC2A 4PU
United Kingdom

SAGE Publications India Pvt. Ltd.
M-32 Market
Greater Kailash I
New Delhi 110 048 India

Printed in the United States of America

Morris, Lynn Lyons
    How to measure performance and use tests / Lynn Lyons Morris,
Carol Taylor Fitz-Gibbon, Elaine Lindheim.
        p.   cm.—(Program evaluation kit (2nd ed.); 7)
    Bibliography: p.
    Includes index.
    ISBN 0-8039-3132-8 (pbk.)
        1. Universities and colleges—Examinations. 2. Academic
    achievement. I. Fitz-Gibbon, Carol Taylor. II. Lindheim, Elaine.
    III. Title. IV. Series
    LB2366.M66   1987
    378'.1664—dc19   87-21771   CIP

96 97 98 99 00 01 19 18 17 16 15 14

CONTENTS

Acknowledgments

The preparation of this second edition of the Center for the Study of Evaluation *Program Evaluation Kit* has been a challenging task, made possible only through the combined efforts of a number of individuals. First and foremost, Drs. Lynn Lyons Morris and Carol Taylor Fitz-Gibbon, the authors and editor of the original Kit. Together, they authored all eight of the original volumes, an enormous undertaking that required incredible knowledge, dedication, persistence, and painstaking effort. Lynn also worked relentlessly as editor of the entire set. Having struggled through only a revision, I stand in great awe of Lynn's and Carol's enormous accomplishment. This second edition retains much of their work and obviously would not have been possible without them.

Thanks also are due to Gene V Glass, Ernie House, Michael Q. Patton, Carol Weiss, and Robert Boruch, who reviewed our plans and offered specific assistance in targeting needed revisions. The work would not have proceeded without Marvin C. Alkin, who planted the seeds for the second edition and collaborated very closely during the initial planning phases.

I would like to acknowledge especially the contribution and help of Michael Q. Patton. True to form, Michael was an excellent, utilization-focused formative evaluator for the final draft manuscript, carefully responding to our work and offering innumerable specific suggestions for its improvement. We have incorporated into the *Handbook* his framework for differentiating among kinds of evaluation studies (formative, summative, implementation, outcomes).

Many staff members at the Center for the Study of Evaluation contributed to the production of the Kit. The entire effort was supervised by Aeri Lee, able office manager at the Center. Katherine Fry, word processing expert, was able to accomplish incredible graphic feats for the *Handbook* and tirelessly labored on manuscript production and data transfer. Ruth Paysen, who was a major contributor to the production of the original Kit, also was a painstaking and dedicated proofreader for the second edition. Margie Franco, Tori Gouveia, and Katherine Lu also participated in the production effort.

Marie Freeman and Pamela Aschbacher, also from the Center, contributed their ideas, editorial skills, and endless examples. Carli

Rogers, of UCLA Contracts and Grants, was both caring and careful in her negotiations for us.

At Sage Publications, thanks to Sara McCune for her encouragement and to Mitch Allen for his nudging and patience.

And at the Center for the Study of Evaluation, the project surely would not have been possible without Eva L. Baker, Director. Eva is a continuing source of encouragement, ideas, support, fun, and friendship.

—Joan L. Herman
Center for the Study of Evaluation
University of California, Los Angeles

Chapter 1
Measuring Performance for Program Evaluation: Preliminary Considerations

The purpose of this book is to help you determine how well the program you are evaluating has met performance *objectives*—usually those mentioned in the program's official description but possibly others added to your measurement plan for one reason or another.[1] The book intends to support you toward this aim in two ways: (1) It provides suggestions, procedures, and rules of thumb for performing evaluation tasks related to measuring performance for program evaluation; and (2) it introduces some of the *theory* underlying the procedures for developing and selecting performance tests and interpreting their results.

Evaluators in a variety of settings, ranging from school-based educational programs to health, human services, and business-oriented training programs, need to know how to measure performance. The theoretical portions of this book (for example, the chapters on test construction and the validity and reliability of performance instruments) apply equally to all settings where you may be called upon to measure performance. Certain of the application topics, however, may be of more interest to you in some settings than in others. For instance, when you are evaluating a school program you will need to be familiar with standardized norm-referenced achievement tests, a topic that will be of less concern to you when you are evaluating on-the-job training programs.

The book's contents are based on the experience of evaluators at the Center for the Study of Evaluation, University of California, Los Angeles, on advice from experts in the field of educational measurement, and on the comments of people who used the original field test edition. Wherever possible, procedures are presented in a step-by-step format. This should give you maximum practical help with minimum theoretical clutter. Keep in mind, however, that many of the recommended procedures described in this book are methods for selecting, administering, and interpreting measures *under the most advantageous circumstances.* Since few evaluation situations will exactly match those envisioned here, however, *you should not expect to be able to duplicate exactly the suggestions in the book.* It is hoped that you will examine the principles and examples provided, and adapt them to the press of your own time constraints, the context of your evaluation, and your data requirements.

An underlying purpose of this book is to help you, through your own work, to improve practice in the field of evaluation. While most evaluations fall short of providing absolutely clear information on the worth of programs or program components, the task of any one evaluator is to provide the best information possible. This means gathering the most highly credible information allowable within the constraints of your situation and presenting the information to each of your evaluation audiences[2] in a form that makes it useful to them. Your task with respect to the program's performance goals is *to provide each audience with descriptions of the degree of success the program seems to have produced, supported by evidence that the performance measures you have used are sensitive to the program's outcomes and likely to be giving you accurate information.*

Each of the book's chapters deals with one area of practical advice. Chapter 1 presents an overview of the various strategies you can use to systematically measure the attainment of performance objectives. These strategies are suitable for use with knowledge, skill, and behavioral outcomes. The strategies can be used when evaluating educational achievement. They also can be utilized in the evaluation of health education programs, human services interventions, and business training programs. The principles discussed throughout the book are intended to be general enough to be applicable in almost any situation where information about performance is collected and reported.

Chapters 2 and 3 deal with locating and selecting published tests. Chapter 2 describes the types of performance tests that might already be available—from commercially published instruments, curriculum embedded tests, and state- or local-mandated measures. Chapter 3 provides assistance in determining the appropriateness of an existing instrument for measuring performance. It presents a Table for Program-

Test Comparison (Table 6). Following a step-by-step procedure to complete the table, you will be able to calculate indices of relative test appropriateness to the program you are evaluating. These indices show the match between the test and the program's most important objectives, the proportion of these objectives that the test covers, and the proportion of the test's items that are relevant to the program.

For some evaluations you might need to construct a new test. Chapter 4 describes the basic steps in developing a performance measure. It also presents references on the topics of test construction and item writing. Chapters 5 and 6 deal with the technical quality and use of tests. Chapter 5 discusses reliability and validity issues in performance testing. Chapter 6 contains a short discussion of test interpretation and score reporting.

Evaluator Roles

The *Program Evaluation Kit*, of which this book is one component, is intended for use primarily by people conducting *program* evaluations. As a program evaluator, the amount of effort you invest in selecting, constructing, administering, and scoring performance instruments—as well as the amount of information you will need to collect concerning each instrument's measurement accuracy—will be largely determined by the *role* you play with respect to the program being evaluated. Your job will take on one of two shapes, depending on the task you have been assigned. In some cases you may find that you are to assume some of the duties of each:

(1) You may have responsibility for producing a *summary statement* about the effectiveness of the program. In this case you probably will deliver a report to the program's overseers, its funding agency, a government office, or another representative of the program's constituency. In this report you will probably be expected to describe the program, to produce a statement of its goals, to estimate the extent to which these goals have been achieved, to note unanticipated outcomes that the program seems to have produced, and possibly to compare it with alternative programs. If this description fits your job, you are a *summative evaluator*.

(2) Your evaluation task may assign you the role of *helper* or *advisor* to program planners and developers. You may then be called upon to examine the program as it develops, identify areas where it needs improvement, spot potential problems, describe for the benefit of the staff the nature of program activities, and perhaps periodically test participants' progress in achieving cognitive, attitudinal, or other

performance goals. In this situation you have many jobs, all demanding that you work with the project staff to help them produce the best possible program. You may or may not be required to write a report. If this loosely defined job role seems closer to yours, then you are a *formative evaluator*.

The information about the design, administration, and interpretation of performance measures contained in this book is intended for use by both formative and summative evaluators. Your perspective on the measurement of performance will vary, however, depending on which of the two roles is yours.

The Perspective of the Summative Evaluator

The summative evaluator's primary interest is to find and use instruments that measure whether the program obtained *its overall goals*. For this reason, if you are a summative evaluator, you must pay close attention to the program's announced and apparent performance objectives. You will be interested in designing or purchasing measures that are most sensitive to determining the accomplishment of these objectives. The summative evaluator's interest in describing the program's overall impact on performance should extend, as well, to a concern for measuring outcomes that seem to be occurring but that program designers have not mentioned among their objectives.

As a summative evaluator, you may have additional reasons for measuring performance. If you are using an evaluation *design* to determine the extent to which good outcomes can be attributed solely to the program, then you may wish to use a performance test for assigning participants to program or comparison groups.[3] This common use of performance information, called *blocking* or *stratified sampling*, ensures that the groups produced will be, at the outset, as alike in prior characteristics as possible.

The summative evaluator may receive a request to include in the final report not only a statement of the program's attainment of its own objectives, but also an indication of how participants in the program now compare in their performance with people in other programs. In these cases, the evaluator needs to select, administer, and report the results of tests that provide such normative data.

Because a summative evaluation report could affect important decisions about the program's future, you need to ensure *high credibility* in the instruments you select or develop. That is, you must use instruments that your evaluation audiences regard as appropriate and accurate.

The Perspective of the Formative Evaluator

By contrast, the formative evaluator's reasons for measuring performance are less official. Usually, if you are a formative evaluator, your major responsibility concerning performance measures is to make *progress checks* throughout the course of the program and to ensure that participants are learning what is expected and keeping to the anticipated pace. The primary audience for this information is the program's staff and planners. Because of their intimacy with the program, staff members will usually not insist on elaborate demonstrations of the technical excellence of the instrument, though of course they will want to be able to trust what it tells them.

Another task of the formative evaluator may be to conduct short experiments to try out program components or to settle controversies among planners about which versions of program implementation will work best. In these situations you will select or construct tests that measure the *specific objectives* of the components under scrutiny.

Because of less rigid data collection requirements, the formative evaluator can be more flexible than the summative evaluator in choosing or developing performance instruments. The *end-of-unit tests* that often accompany curriculum materials, for instance, are usually suspect as measures of program achievement for the purpose of summative evaluation because such tests may too narrowly focus on the particular program materials used. Consumers of summative information generally want to know whether the program has achieved outcomes that can be successfully used in *other*, nonprogram situations. For formative evaluation, however, unit tests are ideal data collection methods; they tell the staff whether participants are at least learning what the program materials contain. In general, as a *formative evaluator, you can assess performance using whatever method you and your immediate audience perceive as providing credible evidence.* Of course, if you find yourself producing measurement instruments to settle controversies among the staff about alternative ways to implement the program, the need for technically defensible measures will again become critical.

If a *summative* evaluation is in the program's future, then an additional aim of the formative evaluator might be to find or produce performance instruments that have wide credibility, while still presenting a fair picture of the program's effects. To this end, you can collect unit tests, instructor-constructed tests, and instruments from related programs, and should try these out during the course of program development to look for items sensitive to attainment of the particular program's objectives.

As a formative evaluator, you may want to collect data that will *stimulate discussion* among staff members and planners. Monitoring participant progress in achieving program objectives can prod the staff to set more reasonable expectations about what the program can accomplish in the time during which participants are exposed to it. By measuring achievement of outcomes that are *not* mentioned among the program's stated objectives, the formative evaluator can point out where the program is producing unanticipated effects or where it is deflecting attention from another area in which performance may be slipping. The formative evaluator's strongest contribution to the program could turn out to be the discovery of important skills necessary to program success—skills that the program did not take into account— or the identification of abilities that the program indeed produced but that had not been identified as program objectives.

Whether you are reading this book with a formative or summative evaluation in mind—or for professional growth—*How to Measure Performance and Use Tests* should familiarize you with major issues and tasks surrounding the design and use of performance instruments for program evaluation. Should you wish to explore the measurement of performance in greater depth, you will find suggestions for further reading at the end of most chapters.

Measurement Strategies

Performance can be measured in a variety of different ways. As an evaluator, you should be familiar with the range of measurement strategies available, so that you can select or develop the type of instrument best suited to the outcomes you want to assess.

Selected Response Tests

All pencil-and-paper tests where examinees select their answer from among various choices provided fit in this general category. Most common are multiple choice, true and false, and matching items. The majority of performance tests are developed in this format, primarily because of the ease of administering and scoring the measures when large numbers of examinees are to be evaluated under standardized conditions.

Constructed Response Tests

When examinees have to compose an answer to a question—for example, write a short answer, solve a problem or deliver an oral presentation—the test is classified as having a constructed response format. One area where constructed response tests have become increasingly popular is the direct assessment of writing ability. Examinees are asked to display their writing ability by composing letters, paragraphs and short essays, rather than by answering selected response questions about grammar, correct usage, and so on.

Constructed response tests are more difficult to score than selected response measures, primarily because there is no single "correct" answer. In order to use a constructed response test for program evaluation, explicit scoring criteria must be developed and raters trained and monitored in the consistent application of those standards. Constructed response measures often require a greater investment of time and resources to administer. In most situations, however, the gains resulting from a test that more closely approximates the actual performance skill being measured outweigh the increased time and costs associated with scoring.

Work Simulations

Work simulations are a possible type of performance test for job-related training and other programs. A simulation requires respondents to perform under controlled conditions similar to those found in real-life situations. Examples of work simulations include "in-box" exercises to test managers' decision-making skills and flight simulations to test pilots' navigational skills.

Work Sample Tests

Another way to evaluate the success of training programs in developing work skills is through observations of on-the-job performance. In a work sample test, trainees complete a series of tasks under actual rather than simulated work conditions, with observers rating the job performance. In order to make work samples a valid and reliable form of performance assessment, clear operational definitions of the desired behaviors need to be developed, observers must be carefully trained, a variety of settings must be sampled, and more than one observer should be used.

Self-Report Measures

Some types of performance are well suited to measurement through self-report. In this type of assessment, respondents provide information about the degree to which behaviors of interest are occurring. The types of behavior promoted by health education programs offer an example of the use of self-report measures of performance. A health promotion program, for example, might have as its overall goal that participants follow a healthier life-style. This might include exercising regularly, eating a nutritionally sound diet, and reducing stress. Self-report measures for this program might ask respondents to indicate their exercise patterns over a period of time, list the foods eaten during the past week, and describe instances when stress management techniques were or were not utilized.

While self-report measures are relatively easy to develop and administer, they do raise the concern that respondents may report what they believe to be the socially desirable behavior. Methods for at least partially countering this tendency include having respondents remain anonymous, using identification schemes such as numbers rather than names to account for program participants, and including a statement in the directions that makes clear there are no right or wrong answers.

Performance Indicators

This type of measurement requires you as the evaluator to establish indicators that can be used to demonstrate participants' success in attaining program objectives. For example, participants in a training program for word processing operators might be evaluated by determining the speed and accuracy with which they can enter various types of text. Participants in a customer relations training program might be judged on the number of telephone inquiries they handle within a specified time period. And sales trainees might be evaluated on the number of sales they make on the job.

Extant Data

A final strategy you may wish to consider when measuring performance is the use of extant data. To use this measurement strategy, you will need to identify information that has been collected for other purposes and that might be relevant for the evaluation you are conducting. Then you must develop a plan for obtaining this information. In some instances, it may be necessary to review existing records in order to extract the pertinent data. In other instances, the data may be available simply for the asking. For example, state assessment results are usually fairly easily obtained and often pertinent for use in program evaluation. Public records offer another source of extant data. You might review the charts kept by a public health clinic, for example, in order to determine the number of children immunized at the clinic. These data could then be used to evaluate the effectiveness of a health promotion campaign aimed at getting parents to bring their children in for their immunizations. In a business setting, an employee program aimed at improving worker morale might be evaluated in part by consulting personnel records to determine the level of absenteeism or the turnover rate at the worksite.

Two Major Approaches to Testing

In addition to being familiar with the range of assessment strategies available for measuring performance, you need also to be aware of two quite different approaches that are used in developing and interpreting all performance tests. A test can be constructed so that it is either *norm-referenced* or *criterion-referenced.* A norm-referenced test provides information about how examinees perform relative to other examinees. A criterion-referenced test provides information about how examinees perform relative to a specified standard or criterion of performance. In order to understand the key differences between these two approaches to assessment, an appropriate place to begin is with some background historical information.

How Norm- and Criterion-Referenced Tests Came About

The first tests used on a large scale and developed systematically were *norm*-referenced. They were used for sorting people into, say, IQ groups and infantry and officer candidate school nominees. For the purpose of this discussion the primary distinctive feature of these tests was their method of scoring—scores were relative. Since the purpose of the test was to compare people, simply knowing that Recruit Burns got 32 items right was not helpful. So the tests were *normed*; that is, they were administered to large groups of people and the distribution of their scores was graphed. Knowing how a norm group would score enabled test developers to convert "32 right" to a standard, comparative score. If, for instance, 75% of the norm group had scored lower than 32, then

Burns scored at the 75th percentile. For choosing and sorting people, this is more useful information.

The *method of development* of norm-referenced tests (NRTs) was determined by their use. They needed to discriminate among people. Typically, the process of developing an NRT went—and still goes—something like this:

(1) A broad and general area of human performance is chosen as the topic of the test. Usually this topic area, or "construct," is reflected in the test's title: *Academic Attainment, Scholastic Aptitude, Modern Language Proficiency, Manual Dexterity.*

(2) To ensure that the test covers the construct's major manifestations or adequately represents curricula in widespread use, the test developers survey the subject content and arrive at a range of cognitive or affective behaviors that can be formed into test items. A *content/process matrix* is frequently used to organize this survey of possible kinds of items and to focus attention on how many items—and therefore how much weight—should be assigned to each sub-area of the construct. An example of a content/process matrix used to plan a unit test in Spanish is presented in Table 1. It shows the various topics covered by the test and the relative emphasis given to each.

(3) For each sort of item called for in the plan, a large number of candidate items is written.

(4) Items are tried out on an appropriate group of examinees, and item statistics are computed. Each item included on the final version of the test is required to do its part to produce scores that rank people. Statistical methods of item analysis are generally used to eliminate items that decrease the efficiency of the test in producing this ranking. The difficulty index,[4] calculated per item, allows the test developer to weed out items that too many people pass or fail, and retain those passed by close to half of the examinees. Good *item discrimination* is another property that norm-referenced test developers want their instruments to have. An item discrimination index[5] shows to what extent high achievers on the test did better on a given item than low achievers did. In order to locate flaws in multiple-choice items, test developers may check to see which of the incorrect alternatives were avoided by most or all of the examinees.

With the rise of individualized instruction in the 1960s, curriculum designers discovered that they needed tests for monitoring the progress of the students. In order to allow a student to progress through a program of instruction, educators wanted to know at various junctures precisely *what the student knew*, and whether he or she knew *enough* to go on. This would mean meeting a standard or criterion level of performance.

TABLE 1
Content/Process Matrix for a Test in Spanish

PROCESSES

CONTENTS	Listening & Translation to spoken English	Listening & Response in spoken Spanish	Reading & Translation to written Spanish	Reading & Response in written Spanish	Reading & Translation to written English	TOTAL
Expressions of quantity	1 #B-1*	2 #B-4, B-5	2 #A-1, A-2		1 #A-22	6
Time of day	1 #B-2	2 #B-6, B-7	2 #A-3, A-4		1 #A-23	6
Dates	1 #B-3	2 #B-8, B-9	2 #A-5, A-6		1 #A-24	6
Usage: por/para			2 #A-7, A-8			2
Usage: ser/estar		2 #B-10, B-11	3 #A-9, A-10, A-11	2 #A-16, A-17		7
Number and person: gustar		1 #B-12	1 #A-12	1 #A-18	1 #A-25	4
Idioms with hacer, tener, poner			3 #A-13, A-14, A-15	3 #A-19, A-20, A-21	3 #A-26, A-27, A-28	9
TOTAL	3	9	15	6	7	40

*Cells show number of items and item numbers for each area of content which the test measures.

It became clear to a number of people, notably Glaser (1963),[6] that the techniques for generating NRTs were unsuited to this purpose. For one thing, they were not designed to examine *the amount of subject matter known*; they were intended to decide how well a student's general academic performance compared with that of other students. They were *referenced* primarily to the *norm* group, and only secondarily to the *subject area.*

Because of this, NRTs had two more specific problems as well:

(1) The presence of items that were good discriminators, while considered a great asset of NRTs, could penalize a student who had learned well enough to progress further in the curriculum but not so well as to overcome the *trickiness* in some NRT items. Some measurement experts felt, in fact, that item selection procedures based on discrimination indices for NRTs had removed just the sort of straightforward items that one would want a unit test to contain.

(2) The rather loosely constructed content/process matrix method for designing NRTs made it difficult to say exactly what respondents who did well actually knew. They knew a little of this and a little of that; but did passing a proficiency test in Spanish, for instance, mean that they could correctly conjugate the language's most commonly used irregular verbs? NRT scores were inadequate for determining conclusively whether students had learned *specific* skills.

In the late 1960s, test designers began to produce tests to help educators detect what students had learned in given subject areas. Since these tests would be used to determine whether students had *mastered* specific instructional objectives, the tests were called *criterion-referenced*. Students passed them by attaining or surpassing the score pre-set as the *criterion* of sufficient knowledge or skill.

Of course, classroom teachers have informally made both criterion- and norm-referenced interpretations of tests for a long time. A teacher, for example, may have given a 20-item spelling test. If the teacher decided that the top 10% of the class should get A's, then he was using a norm-referenced interpretation. If he decided that any student who misspelled fewer than three words should receive an A, his interpretation was based on a performance criterion. What has been noteworthy about criterion-referenced testing (CRT) is its development of techniques for designing and using CRTs more effectively *on a large scale* and for purposes, such as statewide competency testing and professional certificating, that transcend the individual classroom.

The desire to set criteria of proficiency in particular skill areas led to new approaches to test *construction.* If test scores were to show specifically what program participants had learned, test developers would need methods for planning tests that were much more detailed than the content/process matrix. This led measurement experts to the concept of *domain-referenced* testing. A domain-referenced test is one that is assembled by sampling in a prescribed way from a well-defined set of items that measure a performance outcome. One advantage of using such a test is that it provides a clear means of generalizing about what an examinee knows. If Alisa gets three out of four items right on a domain-referenced test, we are justified in saying that she could get about three out of every four items right on all items from the same behavioral *domain,* that is, from the class of all items that *could* have been on the test as described in the *domain of test specifications.*

Criterion-referenced test specifications prescribe the exact nature of the items that are candidates for the test. This prescription includes

- instructions to the examinee and other conditions surrounding test administration,
- the extent to which item components may vary, down to details of permissible vocabulary, formats, and the characteristics of distracters for multiple-choice items, and
- objective scoring procedures, if the test calls for a constructed response.[7]

During test tryouts, item selection depends on pass or fail patterns only to the extent that items that respondents *do not understand* are discarded or revised so that they become comprehensible.

NRTs and CRTs for Program Evaluation

The growing consensus among evaluators is that, in general, criterion-referenced tests serve formative evaluation purposes better than do norm-referenced tests. Norm-referenced tests are useful for gaining indications of the *overall* performance of students, but they fail to reveal strong and weak points in instruction—information that is usually of interest to the formative evaluator and may concern the summative as well. While norms are extremely useful in some evaluation situations—most often summative—where you might want to compare program students' performance with external comparison groups, norm-referenced tests have been criticized as being insensitive to some of the gains that students make through program participation.

In general, a *norm-referenced* test will serve your evaluation purpose in the following situations:

- if you are seeking to select program participants and need a test that differentiates among people;
- if you wish to match or block students, classrooms, or schools prior to assigning them to a program, and you want to base this matching on measures of general ability or comparative achievement;
- if you plan to use test results to compare performance of program participants with that of a nationwide or local norm group.

When you want a test that will be maximally sensitive to the changes in performance brought about by the program, then you are advised to consider using a criterion-referenced test keyed to the program's objectives. There are myriad reasons for this advice. One is that regardless of the relevance of some of its items to the program, a norm-referenced test usually has to be administered in its entirety in order for you validly to interpret scores in the manner described in the test manual. On the other hand, criterion-referenced tests are designed to be broken into parts according to the objectives that the items measure, so you can freely pick and choose items with no loss in interpretability of results.

Another reason for using CRTs in program evaluation is that some NRT items that discriminate well among students tend to be "oddballs." They contain some twist that students who know the material might still fail to see. This criticism is an attack on the validity of using the norm-referenced test for determining what students understand or can do. Presumably, then, NRTs might be measuring something else in addition to the objectives described in the test manual. Some writers have speculated that this "something else" is *test wiseness* or a certain kind of cleverness that picks up cues that are independent of the content or skills on which the test should focus. Also, where students have equal proficiency in a subject, it will be the quicker and brighter students who complete more items accurately. Some critics of NRTs have gone so far as to claim that the reliability and validity of norm-referenced achievement tests derive in large part from the contribution that general ability makes to test results.

Not all experts agree with the criticisms leveled against norm-referenced tests. Proponents of norm-referenced tests argue that while items are ultimately selected for their ability to discriminate among students, the discrimination provided by the test enables it to distinguish students who have learned the subject well from those whose knowledge is so weak that they must go slowly.

While the controversy over the various advantages of criterion- and norm-referenced tests continues to rage, many evaluators choose criterion-referenced tests where possible. In situations where it is important to know in detail *what* students can do and *what* they cannot do, criterion-referenced tests simply yield clearer information.

Some Critical Questions

The major reason why a program evaluator—either formative or summative—measures performance is because the evaluation audience is concerned about whether the program is meeting written or unwritten performance *objectives*. Before you make any decisions about *how* to collect your information, therefore, you will need to examine these performance objectives in the light of the following questions, each of which raises issues that must be considered before you proceed.

Question 1. What use will be made of the performance information?

Your answer to this question will determine the amount of time and effort you should spend on measuring performance. If you are a formative evaluator, ask yourself whether program staff or planners are indeed committed to making program changes based on your evaluation. Will program alterations result from the findings you report about participant progress or from short experiments you are able to conduct? Will people be willing to discuss and take note of the performance information you provide? In other words, will the information you supply make a difference?

The summative evaluator should consider *who* will read the evaluation report and what this audience will do with the information. Could the summative information reach a publication such as a newspaper? Might it be used as an ax to eliminate the program or as a promotional wedge to increase its acceptance? Or has past experience shown that summative evaluation for this particular evaluation audience is merely *pro forma?*

Of course, prior to reporting your information, you can never be completely sure about how it will be used. On the other hand, you cannot help but use a projection of its influence to determine whether you should invest more or less effort in measuring performance.

For one thing, anticipation about the potential influence of the information will affect decisions about whether to seek new and better measures or use available tests and easily obtained information. If you discover that your measure of the attainment of program objectives could result in drastic changes or even termination of the program, then you must make a commitment to find or construct a measure that is not only valid and technically acceptable, but that also measures the outcomes *fairly*. A measure that is *fair to the program* is one that is relevant to the major information, skills, or attitudes addressed by the program *as it was actually implemented.* However, in summative evaluations where the program's planners and staff have promised a program that would accomplish a set of predetermined objectives—say, to raise reading level by a certain amount within two years—*fairness to the program's constituency* requires that *these* outcomes be a primary focus of the evaluation.

Question 2. What outcomes will guide selection or construction of the performance measure?

In order to be useful as a reference for selecting a test or as underlying organizers for constructing one, objectives need to meet the following four criteria:

   A. Objectives should be clearly stated. Of course, *how clearly* depends on whether you will use them for test selection or test construction. Objectives used to guide test selection should be stated precisely enough so that it will be clear which tests more nearly measure the skills addressed by your particular program. If the objectives will be used to underpin *construction* of the test, then they must meet more stringent criteria—they should be described clearly enough that several test item writers working from the outcome descriptions would produce nearly identical test questions.

   There are several places where you might locate objectives adequate to guide a search for the appropriate performance measure. If you are evaluating an educational program, one approach is to examine the *written instructional materials* being used. Publishers often preface these with lists of objectives and detailed curriculum outlines. Another source of outcomes is the program descriptions developed by program planners.

   In some cases, you may wish to *write the outcome statements yourself.* If time is short, if the program's subject matter is highly specialized, or if your assessment will be fairly informal, this may be the best strategy. A few interviews with the program planners and a look at the program in action should give you a good idea of the objectives toward which the program is aimed.

   B. In order to produce a test that is relevant to the program, outcomes should be verified against the program's implementation. Programs that aim toward many objectives often put into practice activities to accomplish only some of them. In most cases, before choosing a test, you should be careful to distinguish between the objectives actively pursued and other "official" objectives that for one reason or another have been shelved. The long lists of ambitious objectives that accompany official statements of programs are often written because program planners have prepared a proposal for a funding agency. Such proposals need to promise great things in order to be placed in contention for funding. Sometimes, too, highly ambitious outcomes are symptomatic of the aspirations of naive planners. Once a program has been implemented, harsh reality forces the staff to reduce the number or difficulty of the objectives on which teaching efforts will focus. By looking at the program in operation and discussing the outcomes you plan to measure with the program staff and possibly even with participants, you should be better able to find a test that assesses the gains of the program that actually occurred.

Even when your purpose as *summative* evaluator is to produce a test that matches the program's "official" objectives, you should not ignore program implementation. The program should be given a chance to look as good as it can in achieving those objectives it does address.

C. Outcomes should reflect the level of performance that the program hopes to produce. How an outcome is phrased is critical for test selection or construction. The skill represented by a general program outcome can be mastered at different depths. These different levels of expertise will result in the display of increasingly complex test behavior. If the level of performance is specified in the outcome, then the test items should call for correspondingly appropriate responses. Too often outcomes describing a program define skills at a lower or higher level than they are actually taught in the program.

For example, a science program may be attempting to teach basic concepts at an elementary level:

> When asked, the student will express that photosynthesis is the method by which plants nourish themselves.

Then again, if the curriculum aims toward more complex skills, the science program may want to produce deeper understanding:

> The student will write an essay describing the conditions under which photosynthesis occurs.

The program might even seek to develop quite advanced abilities:

The student will describe, via an essay and appropriate equations, the chemical processes occurring during photosynthesis.

Most programs seek to develop various skills and attitudes at different levels of attainment. The Taxonomy of Educational Objectives developed by Bloom et al. (1956) and outlined in annotated form in Table 2, identifies several levels of knowledge and understanding. Someone familiar with the program should review the objectives with such a taxonomy in mind before the objectives are used as a framework for prescribing a performance test.

D. Outcomes that underlie the test should be of high priority. You may find yourself facing long lists of objectives. Many programs, particularly those educational programs involving design of an extensive curriculum, embody myriad objectives. It is not unusual, in fact, for programs based on installing a commercial curriculum to encompass hundreds of objectives or, where objectives are absent, separate curriculum topics. You of course cannot test all of these, and you need to ensure that the test you do develop or select reflects the program's *major* emphases. If you are a summative evaluator, you need to locate or construct the test that gives you the highest payoff in terms of assessing critical outcomes. If you are a formative evaluator monitoring student progress over the course of the program, you might construct several specific tests to assess separately the development of the skills addressed by the different program units whose quality you want to monitor. On the other hand, much like a summative evaluator, you might construct one general test that could be given repeatedly to monitor overall progress in student performance. If a program has few high priority objectives but still more than you feel you will be able to test, then consider sampling outcomes.

Shrinking the set of objectives through ranking or sampling. Table 3 gives a short description of four prioritization and sampling methods to consider as a means to deal with objectives when they are too numerous and/or when their relative importance to the program in question is unknown.

Methods 1 and 2 both guide you in assigning priorities. Method 1 produces a list of objectives prioritized by means of one or another rating procedure. Rating can be based on either a "retrospective needs assessment" or an analysis of the relative emphases given to different objectives by the program *as implemented.* Retrospective needs assess-

TABLE 2
An Annotated Cognitive Domain Taxonomy*

This classification describes, from simplest to most complex, six degrees to which information that is taught can be learned.

1. **Knowledge.** *Recalling information pretty much as it was learned.*
   In its simplest manifestation, this includes knowledge of the terminology and specific facts—dates, people, etc.—associated with an area of subject matter. At a more complex level it means knowing the major sub-areas, methods of inquiry, classifications and ways of thinking characteristic of the subject area, as well as its central theories and principles.

2. **Comprehension.** *Reporting information in a way other than how it was learned in order to show that it has been understood.*
   Most basically this means reporting something learned through an alternative medium. More complex evidence of comprehension involves interpreting information in "one's own words" or in some other original way, or extrapolating from it to new but related ideas and implications.

3. **Application.** *Use of learned information to solve a problem.*
   This means carrying over knowledge of facts or methods learned in one specific context to completely new ones.

4. **Analysis.** *Taking learned information apart.*
   Analysis means figuring out a subject matter's most elemental ideas and their interrelationships.

5. **Synthesis.** *Creating something new—and good, based on some criterion.*
   This creation can be something that communicates to an audience, that plans a successful goal-directed endeavor, or that subsumes a collection of ideas within a new theory.

6. **Evaluation.** *Judging the value of something for a particular purpose.*
   This means making a statement of something's worth based either on one's own well-developed criteria or on the well-understood criteria of another.

*Adapted from *TAXONOMY OF EDUCATIONAL OBJECTIVES: The Classification of Educational Goals: HANDBOOK 1: Cognitive Domain*, by Benjamin S. Bloom et al. Copyright © 1956 by Longman Inc.

ment is a fancy term that means that concerned people—usually the evaluation's audience and program planners—are asked for their opinions about what the program should accomplish. Since these opinions are based on the raters' values and personal views toward the program's subject matter and goals, objectives prioritization via this method usually results in measurements based on the program's ability to prepare participants to function within a broader context—in a higher grade, on the job, whatever. Rating based on the program-as-implemented, on the other hand, focuses the evaluation on how well the program is achieving whatever it seems to be trying hardest to accomplish. A test based on these objectives gives the program its best chance to show positive effects. Raters asked to examine objectives for program relevance should be, of course, as familiar as possible with what the program *looks like in action.*

To the extent that the program in operation addresses the objectives of its constituency and planners, the lists of important outcomes produced by the two rating methods will coincide. Retrospective needs assessment and program implementation are presented separately, however, because the relative orderings of objectives produced by the two seldom do correspond.

Method 2 in Table 3 for reducing the size of a pool of objectives uses *objectives hierarchies*—logically derived learning or task sequences that point out key objectives.

Methods 3 and 4 use sampling. Following Method 3, you would take a simple random sample of objectives. Because of the importance of choosing the right objectives to guide *test selection*, Methods 1, 2, and 3 are discussed more fully in Chapter 3 (pages 45 to 65).

Method 4, matrix sampling, is *not* a procedure for reducing the size of an objectives pool. Rather, it is a technique for testing *many* objectives by giving different sets of items to different groups of participants. Each participant does not, therefore, answer every question.[8]

Broadening the set of objectives by attending to generalization and transfer. Besides narrowing the pool of objectives underlying the test, consider expanding it. You might decide to look at objectives that reflect the development of skills *beyond those* specifically addressed by the program. Formulating objectives that describe skills somewhat peripheral to the program's focus or slightly in advance of those outlined by the program might help you demonstrate to the evaluation audience that the program has a relationship to participants' learning performance, or other outcomes *in the future* or *in related skill areas.*

What is more, a list of generalization and transfer objectives should broaden the criteria available to you for selecting a test. The rationale for this advantage goes something like this: Selecting a test to measure program objectives demands that you match test items with expressed

TABLE 3
Solutions to the Problem of Too Many Objectives

Method	Quick Summary	Advantages	Disadvantages	Recommendations
1. Assigning priorities to all objectives through ratings	A group of approximately 15 raters rate all objectives according to a 5-point scale. Criteria determining ratings can vary. Mean ratings determine priorities.	• Yields accurate assessment of the priorities of interest groups represented by the raters. • Involves raters in the evaluation and is therefore likely to increase credibility. • Assures relevance of the evaluation to values and aims of the audiences, and/or to assessing effectiveness of the program *as implemented*.	• Focuses evaluation on a small number of objectives. • Depends on cooperation of raters. • Time-consuming for evaluators and raters.	A good procedure to use, if you have time for it and can gain cooperation from enough raters. Especially recommended when it is deemed crucial that the evaluation show maximum sensitivity to the program as implemented, or to the wants or values of certain groups.
2. Assigning priorities through objectives hierarchies	Objectives grouped into content areas, then charted from simple to complex. The more complex or "terminal" ones receive highest priority.	• Can be done by the evaluator alone—without cooperation from others. • Assigns priority to the most logically complex objectives, avoiding attention to too simple ones.	• Relatively time-consuming, depending on the number of objectives. • It may not be desirable to test only terminal, difficult objectives. • Subject matter may have no inherent hierarchy.	Probably should be used only when you as evaluator must narrow down the number of objectives yourself, without assistance, and when the subject matter lends itself to logical hierarchies.
3. Sampling objectives	Objectives are randomly selected from the total set.	• Can be done by the evaluator alone—without cooperation from others. • The quickest, simplest method. • Treats all program objectives—on the test or not—as instructionally important.	• The risk exists of missing objectives or items that might be important thus reducing the credibility of the evaluation.	Highly recommended when all objectives are of about equal importance
4. Matrix sampling	Many items or objectives are used. They are assigned to parts of a test, and each part is given to different groups of students, usually randomly selected.	• Can be done by the evaluator alone—without cooperation from others. • Many items or objectives are tested, albeit with samples of students rather than all students. • Copying answers not a problem because students take different tests.	• Somewhat involved procedure. • Data not entirely appropriate for use with some statistical tests. • Not practical for group administration with young children who must have the questions read aloud. • Not good for comparing students.	The only method by which you can assess *many* objectives or items. Due to the procedure's complexity, however, use it only when you cannot avoid testing many objectives or items.

program objectives in the hope that you will find a test that is most congruent with your objectives and a minimum of items that test for knowledge or outcomes extraneous to your objectives. If you have specified transfer and generalization objectives, you will be able to perform a more elaborate matching. You will be able to evaluate a given test not only for the information it provides about attainment of the primary outcomes; you will also be able to assess the extent to which its items measure secondary outcomes. The effect of this is simply to give you more information on which to base test selection.

In order to write generalization and transfer objectives, ask yourself or the program planners these questions:

- What skills will be learned *after* the program—skills for which the program supposedly will be preparing participants?
- What particular abilities or outcomes should we be developing in participants that this program might be fostering indirectly?
- What other objectives might likely be attained as a result of participation in this program?
- What longer-term outcomes can be expected by program success?

Question 3. Can you realistically expect that the performance objectives will have been accomplished by the time you plan to do the measuring?

Your answer to this question will determine the degree to which you focus on the processes—activities, materials—of the program in your evaluation in addition to its results or outcomes.

A program's objectives might be so complex or ephemeral that the program, as is, can only hope to *start* participants toward attainment rather than fully accomplish the outcomes within a specified time frame. For example, many advocates of humanistic education maintain that while students in such a program may not in any one semester appear to have learned more subject matter than students in more traditional programs, they actually have begun to learn how to solve problems, how to investigate areas of intellectual endeavor, and how to question and probe. In other words, their learning will eventually show a qualitative and therefore quantitative change; but such change may not be observable for quite some time.

Though your first impulse here—and it's not a bad one—might be to search for tests of creative problem solving, a drawback of such an approach is that probably neither you nor the program planners expect that a short exposure to the program will produce changes so substantial that they will show up on a general standardized test. If, as seems likely, you find no such change, how will you interpret the results? There are two solutions to consider in this situation: (1) Base the evaluation on more immediate and demonstrable objectives, and (2) augment the use of tests with attention to the *processes* that the program has initiated for participants.

The second solution bears some explanation. Though it is important in *any* evaluation to *describe* the program that its participants are experiencing, difficulty with adequately measuring the program's *outcomes* will make proper description of its materials, activities, and administration more important. This situation will require that you design a portion of the evaluation to determine whether the instruction given or program processes implemented adequately reflect the *theory* upon which the program is based. The rationale for this shift in emphasis is a simple one. Money and effort have been invested in the program because people believe that the processes that it includes will bring about the development of the complex performances reflected in its difficult-to-measure objectives.

In this situation, the best use of your time as evaluator will be to monitor whether the program looks and operates as it is supposed to. If you are a summative evaluator, you will tell the funding source whether it got what it paid for. If your function is primarily formative, then you will provide information for keeping the program on track. When you decide to focus on process, the questions you ask about the program will expand from, "Did the program promote the desired performance?" to include "Did the program contain the materials and activities it was supposed to?" You should consult with your evaluation audience before deciding on such a course of action.

If you will be evaluating the program over a long period, say two or three years, an excellent idea is to collect information about changes in, say, creativity or self-direction and to note changes in the same group or across levels over time. After some time, you should start to see effects. In this case, it will be essential that you measure these complex objectives. By this time, the program can be looked upon as a test of whether the activities you have so carefully monitored do indeed bring about the desired outcomes.

Question 4. Do you have available the time and resources to custom-make the test?

In the best of all possible worlds, the best way to assess the attainment of each performance objective is to develop a customized measure—for example, write for it valid items (five or more of them so that your measure is reliable) and administer a test made of these items to every person participating in the program. This will allow you to tell your audience about the degree of achievement of every objective. If you can match this ideal, then you are in a position to produce a highly credible assessment of program effects. Chapter 4 of this book, "Constructing a Test for Program Evaluation," will help you develop such a measure.

Custom-construction of a valid and reliable test, however, is a task beyond the resources of many small-scale evaluations. In these cases, time, convenience, and your own concern for accurate measurement and credibility may dictate that you either purchase a test or use the results from one that is given as a matter of course. If you need to select a test, it is suggested that you use a formal procedure like the one outlined in Chapter 3 to compare tests. This standardized, step-by-step procedure will ensure that you look at each test carefully, basing your choice on the match between its items and the objectives whose achievement you have decided to assess.

If you are a formative evaluator, your selection of a measurement instrument need not be so formal. Your task, in part, is to determine the effectiveness of particular *sub-units* of the program. For this job, you can use unit tests or tests created by the staff or teachers of the program. You might even construct tests by sampling items from practice exercises. Though you may want to use Chapters 2 and 3 to choose and evaluate the tests you will use, many of the problems of the summative evaluator when selecting a measurement instrument—selecting appropriate items for *general* learning or other performance outcomes and representing the overall effect of the program—might not concern you.

If you are a summative evaluator, you will first want to search out published tests that might be useful for your evaluation, since their measurement properties have been established. The introductory pages of Chapter 2 should help you find tests and order specimen sets. Then follow the program-test match procedure in Chapter 3 to help you assess the closeness of fit between the tests you have located and the program you are evaluating. If you can find no tests that seem appropriate, or if the test you select leaves you with a group of high priority objectives that will still not be assessed, you might then attempt to design a short test of your own. Existing tests have the virtue of saving you time and allowing you to use materials that have already been field tested and should therefore be free of major problems. *A good rule of thumb is to use the best of what has already been developed instead of starting from scratch.*

Things to Remember

In summary, this chapter has called your attention to several matters pertinent to selecting or constructing a performance test:

(1) the need to consider how test data will be used;
(2) the need to develop and clarify your performance objectives before attempting to make decisions about how you will measure them;
(3) the need to assure that the performance objectives reflect the level of skill attainment that the program is intended to produce so that you will not find yourself evaluating a program aimed at high-level concept attainment on the basis of whether it communicated simple vocabulary;
(4) the need to decide on the relative importance of performance objectives so that you will be able to focus on those of highest priority;
(5) the need to determine whether performance objectives are likely to be accomplished within the time frame of the evaluation so that you know whether to focus on outcomes or processes or perhaps both;
(6) the need to decide how much of your performance test will be selected from existing measures and how much you will construct yourself with the caveat that you should select existing measures whenever possible.

These reminders apply in practically any measurement situation. They can be summed up in one word: *relevance*. The measure you produce must focus on the same material as does the program's instruction. Technical quality of the test as discussed in Chapter 5 only helps you to estimate the accuracy of whatever measures you choose. The first and most critical step in providing your evaluation with a good performance measure is deciding *what* you want to measure.

Notes

1. Any one of a number of situations could prompt you to measure performance objectives other than those mentioned in the official program description. For instance, you might want to look at side effects—attainment of skills related to but not included in the program. You might also decide to check whether participation in the program has brought about a *slowdown* in performance in an area *not* emphasized by the program.

2. *Audience* is an important concept in evaluation. Many evaluations have several audiences; every evaluation has at least one. *An audience is a person or group who needs the information from the evaluation for a distinct purpose.* Administrators who want to keep track of program installation because they need to monitor the political climate constitute one potential audience. Curriculum developers who want data about the outcomes of a particular program component compose another. Every audience needs different information; and, it is important to note, *each maintains different criteria for what it will accept as believable, credible information.*

3. Discussion of evaluation designs can be found in most texts on the topic of

educational research. See, in particular, Fitz-Gibbon and Morris (1987b) and also Campbell and Stanley (1966).

4. Item difficulty is *zero* if all the examinees got the item wrong, and it is *one* if all the examinees got the item right. Otherwise, it ranges from .01 to .99, reflecting the proportion of the tryout group that succeeded on the item.

5. There are really several indexes of item discrimination. All can be similarly interpreted, however. The values assumed by an item discrimination index can range from –1, through zero, and on up to +1, just like a correlation coefficient. In fact, the meaning of the index is like that of correlation, since a negative discrimination index for an item tells you that results for that item correlate negatively with performance on the test as a whole. Specifically, those who did well on the entire test tended to get that item *wrong*, while those who did poorly on the test tended to get the item *right*. You can imagine that an item with a negative discrimination index would be an embarrassment to a test writer, since such an item is apparently measuring something different from the test as a whole. A discrimination index of zero is not such good news either, since it means that those who failed the test did just as well in the item as those with the highest scores. In most cases, an item must have a positive discrimination index in order for it to be useful on a test that must differentiate among examinees.

6. See R. Glaser (1963) "Instructional technology and the measurement of learning outcomes." *American Psychologist, 18*: 510-522.

7. Chapter 4, "Constructing a Test Program Evaluation," provides an example of test specifications for a criterion-referenced test.

8. Methods for using these and other procedures for prioritizing and sampling objectives and items can be found in Morris and Fitz-Gibbon (1978).

For Further Reading

Bloom, B. S., Madaus, G. F., & Hastings, J. J. (1981). *Evaluation to improve learning* (1st ed.). New York: McGraw-Hill.

Ebel, R. L. (1979). *Essentials of educational measurement* (3rd ed.). Englewood Cliffs, NJ: Prentice-Hall.

Lindvall, C. M., & Nitko, A. J. (1975). *Measuring pupil achievement and aptitude.* New York: Harcourt Brace Jovanovich.

Mager, R. F. (1975). *Preparing instructional objectives* (2nd ed.). Belmont, CA: Fearon.

Mehrens, W. A., & Lehmann, I. J. (1984). *Measurement and evaluation in education and psychology.* New York: Holt, Rinehart & Winston.

Popham, W. J. (1981). *Modern educational measurement.* Englewood Cliffs, NJ: Prentice-Hall.

Chapter 2
Locating Existing Measures

The purpose of this chapter is to help you find an already published performance measure. The advantages of measuring performance using an already existing measure are that you save time and gain the benefit of other people's experience. Such an instrument has already been to some extent "debugged" and probably carries reliability and validity data. You might also be able to find results from its past administrations in other evaluation reports or in the test's accompanying manual. Observing proper caution, *you can compare these results with your own.*

Finding Tests

Already written tests come from three sources:

(1) The curriculum materials used for the program might be accompanied by pre- or posttests, unit tests or curriculum-embedded progress or mastery tests.
(2) The state, district, or funding agency may administer a test as part of its areawide assessment program.
(3) A test can be purchased from a test publisher or borrowed from a researcher, professional association, or the like.

Any or all of these tests can be fit into your evaluation plans.

What to Do with the Tests That Come with the Program

Criterion-referenced tests are often developed for use in managing educational programs. Such tests allow learners to proceed individually to later units on the basis of a passing score. Failing indicates a need for additional instruction. These tests are of great value to a formative evaluator. They help you to detect whether program instruction is of sufficient quality to allow participants to master the program's own embedded test.

For summative evaluation, however, these tests are usually *not appropriate.* Because the tests are part of the program, their periodic passing does not guarantee that the program as a whole is accomplishing its objectives. The test used for assessing the program's *overall effects* should be a different one—a test purchased or constructed for that purpose and administered, usually as a posttest, to all or a representative sample of program participants. What is more, the *design* underlying your evaluation will prescribe certain times when tests should be administered. This schedule will seldom coincide with the times of administration of curriculum-embedded tests. Even a *time series* evaluation design requires that all participants take tests at the same time, not when they are "ready."[1]

For the purposes of summative evaluation, the tests embedded in the curriculum *are* useful as *program implementation* information—evidence that the program occurred as planned. If you construct your *own* test for measuring overall program effects, tests embedded in the curriculum can be used as a source of suggestions for your test items.

A word should be said, in addition, about using the pretest and posttest that accompany the program as a sole source of summative evaluation information. These tests have credibility problems. If you wish to use them, you will have to anticipate two questions from your audience: (1) *Is the pretest perhaps harder than the posttest?* Although not common, this could occur. This concern can be eliminated by reshuffling the items and retyping the forms. Use the odd-numbered items from both tests as *your* pretest and the even-numbered items as the posttest. (2) *Is the test giving the experimental group an undue advantage because of their greater familiarity with the format used in test items?* You can combat this problem by giving the control group, if there is one, practice with the same response formats, directions, and performance conditions to which the experimental group has been accustomed.

What to Do with a Test That Will Be Administered as a Matter of Course

If a test for statewide or districtwide assessment will be administered to most or all program participants, then you should assess the appropriateness of *this* test for your evaluation before you look for another. If the required test looks as though it could assess many of the major objectives of the program, you may have to look no further.

A procedure for determining the *match* between test items and program objectives, which begins on page 46, Chapter 3, can serve as a guide for evaluating any test you think might be used for the evaluation. If you decide to subject the required test to this scrutiny you might as well locate at least one *other* test to compare with the one you must use. The information you gain from this exercise will help you to evaluate the relative quality and appropriateness of the test that you have been required to use.

Should you find that the required test compares poorly with the program's objectives you could supplement your measurements by giving a more relevant alternate test to a sample of participants. You could also actively advocate a switch to another test. If none of this will work, and you are stuck with the required test, then one method remains for assuring a match between the test and the program: *Extract information about how participants performed on just those test items relevant to the program you are evaluating.* The procedure for extracting such information, though timeconsuming, is straightforward:

(1) Obtain a copy of the test that will be administered, and, if you can, cut up the test and paste each item on a separate card. Otherwise, have the items typed on cards.

(2) Have someone who is familiar with the program sort the items into piles labeled

ENTIRELY	MODERATELY	NOT
RELEVANT	RELEVANT	RELEVANT

(3) Designate the items in the three groups "subtests." Make a list of item numbers for each subtest, and plan to analyze the three subtests separately when the test is scored.

(4) Use as an indicator of program success *the mean score of all participants in the program on the subtest composed of the most relevant items.* Depending on the thoroughness of the score-reporting service you receive, this mean can be calculated in one of two ways:

(a) If time is short, or if the agency scoring the standardized test does not provide an item-by-item breakdown of participants' scores, the relevant test items should be scored by hand *before* the tests are sent off for data processing. Add up item results for each participant in the program on the relevant subtest, and from these scores compute the average score for program participants.

(b) If the agency scoring the test does provide a calculation of "percentage correct" for program participants on each test item, then you may save yourself some trouble by waiting for the printout. When it arrives, list this percentage for each item in the subtest as a decimal (e.g., 83% becomes .83). Just add these decimals to obtain the average raw score of the participants on the subtest.[2]

(5) Similarly, obtain the mean score of program participants on the other two subtests if you want some idea of what transfer of learning may have resulted from the program. That is, the program may have indirectly improved participants' performance on items calling for skills somewhat related to the program, or even outside the primary focus of the program.

If you have available item results from the same test for participants who are *not* receiving any instruction aimed at your program's goals, you should save such data for possible use in making comparisons of results on the three subtests.

If you have an evaluation design that seeks to compare the effectiveness of two programs in teaching goals that are common to both and if these goals are also addressed by items on the test you plan to use, two changes in the procedure are called for:

(1) The three piles for sorting items need to be relabeled as, say,

ENTIRELY RELEVANT TO BOTH PROGRAMS	MODERATELY RELEVANT TO BOTH PROGRAMS	REJECTED

(2) Item results for participants in different programs must be kept separate, so that mean subtest scores can be computed separately for participants in different programs.

The procedure outlined here represents a fair way of using a standardized test to measure the attainment of some program objectives. In many cases, the amount of information it provides will be too incomplete to justify the time and effort involved.

Finding Published Tests

You will quickly discover that the majority of tests on the market are norm-referenced, although increasing numbers of criterion-referenced tests are becoming available. Published tests are almost always *standardized*. By the time they are placed on the market, these tests have completed a development phase during which they were validated on groups of subjects. When you purchase such measures, you will receive a *technical manual* that provides norms or comparative data based on the scores of the tryout group, information about the validity and reliability of the instrument, and instructions for administering, scoring, and interpreting results. This information can often be obtained without commitment to buy the test if you write to the publishers requesting a *specimen set*. Most test publishers charge a small fee for specimen sets that usually consist of a sample copy of the instrument and an accompanying manual. A sample letter requesting specimen sets is provided in Figure 1.

The following section briefly describes several bibliographic sources that could be of use in your search for an existing performance measure. These compendia offer extensive lists of available tests. They name many more than could possibly be listed in this book.

Buros, O. K. (Ed.). (1938-1985). *Mental measurements yearbooks* (Vols. 1-9). Highland Park, NJ: Gryphon Press.

The *Mental Measurements Yearbooks* (*MMY*) are available in the reference section of most college and large public libraries. Their primary intent is to provide information *and critical reviews* for *every* test that is commercially available in English-speaking countries and that is "published as a separate test," that is, not just included somewhere within a journal or book. The critical reviews are "written by testing and subject specialists representing various viewpoints." A paragraph accompanying each test title tells you for whom the test is intended, what scores or ratings it yields, the titles of the subparts (if any), the different forms available, administration time, publishing source, and prices of materials.

The yearbooks also provide a list of new and revised books on testing, as well as references to articles discussing the quality or use of any test.

In 1975, Gryphon Press also published a series of derivative volumes including the following: *Reading tests and reviews*, *Science tests and reviews*, *Social studies tests and reviews*, and *Vocational tests and reviews*. As these titles indicate, the books were compiled from appropriate sections of the *Mental measurements yearbooks*, and from *Tests in print II*.

Mitchell, J. V. Jr. (Ed). (1983). *Tests in print III*. Nebraska: University of Nebraska Press.

This volume differs from the *MMY* in several ways: It contains *no* critical reviews and *no* purchase prices, and it has a master index to the

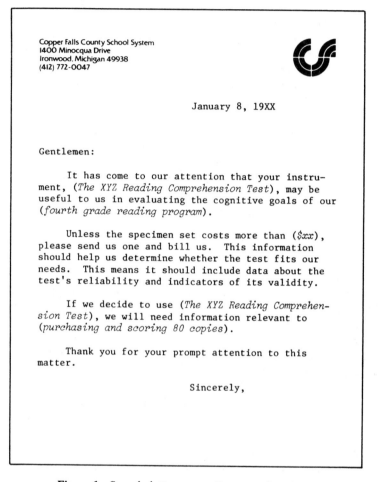

Copper Falls County School System
1400 Minocqua Drive
Ironwood. Michigan 49938
(412) 772-0047

January 8, 19XX

Gentlemen:

It has come to our attention that your instrument, *(The XYZ Reading Comprehension Test)*, may be useful to us in evaluating the cognitive goals of our *(fourth grade reading program)*.

Unless the specimen set costs more than *($xx)*, please send us one and bill us. This information should help us determine whether the test fits our needs. This means it should include data about the test's reliability and indicators of its validity.

If we decide to use *(The XYZ Reading Comprehension Test)*, we will need information relevant to *(purchasing and scoring 80 copies)*.

Thank you for your prompt attention to this matter.

Sincerely,

Figure 1. Sample letter requesting a specimen set

MMY. Like the *MMY*, it describes tests in print by subject area. It points out as well, however, tests of that subject that have gone out of print. Test descriptions, while primarily informational, also include some "statements implying criticism."

The Test Collection. Educational Testing Service, Princeton, NJ, 08541.
The ETS Test Collection has been in existence as a special library since 1967. The collection contains over 10,000 tests. These tests

measure such areas as achievement, aptitude, attitude, interest, personality, sensory-motor skills, and vocational-occupational knowledge. By writing or calling, you can request a brochure that lists 200 test bibliographies that have been compiled according to either subject and age level, type of test, or specific population. Each bibliography includes a minimum of 25 tests and contains annotated entries.

Nafziger, D. H. et al. (1975). *Tests of functional adult literarcy: An evaluation of currently available instruments.* Portland, Oregon: Northwest Regional Educational Laboratory.

This booklet reviews and evaluates 17 tests developed for *adults*, focusing on reading skills crucial for functioning in daily life. The book provides a rationale for the sorts of competencies required by each test. It describes as well the time and materials required, scoring procedures and background information on each test's field testing, revision, or validation. The evaluation section consists of charts that rate each test on 33 criteria. Summary judgments of good, fair, or poor are made in four categories: measurement validity, examinee appropriateness, technical excellence, and administrative usability. The criteria used are explained in the text.

Tests that have subtests are evaluated at the subtest level. Thus the book gives separate evaluations for vocabulary, reading comprehension, spelling, and oral reading. Tests are divided into three categories—those that are "very task oriented and immediately relevant to the examinee's everyday activities," those that are standardized, and those that are informal.

Pletcher, B. P., Locks, N. A., Reynolds, D. F., & Sisson, B. G. (1978). *Guide to assessment instruments for limited-English-speaking students.* New York: Santillana.

As the introduction states, "the reviews contained in this catalogue are designed to be used by school personnel charged with locating and administering appropriate assessment instruments" to students whose first language is Chinese, French, Italian, Navajo, Portuguese, Spanish, or Tagalog, and whose command of English is limited. Each instrument reviewed was either developed or adapted for use with students in grades K-6. All instruments are available to the public and are presently in use somewhere in the United States. None of the instruments included is bound to any particular set of curricular materials, and none is intended to identify developmental or constitutional deficiencies. Information given about each test includes its purpose, score interpretation, grade range, target ethnic group, conditions of administration, reliability and validity, manner of construction and revision, quality of norm scores (if any), and interpretability.

Accompanying each review is a critique of the test's cultural and linguistic appropriateness as judged by a geographically diverse group of educators who are native speakers of "the dialect spoken by the students for whom the instrument was intended."

Almost 100 instruments are reviewed for elementary school students whose first language is Spanish. Of these, 19 are measures of language dominance; 24, of proficiency in written or spoken Spanish; 17, of proficiency in English; 10, of achievement in more than one school subject; 6, of general ability or scholastic aptitude; and 12, of attitude or self-concept.

A total of 12 instruments are reviewed for use with elementary school students whose first language is Navajo, 11 for native speakers of French, 10 for Portuguese, 7 for Chinese, 5 for Tagalog, and 3 for Italian.

Young, M. B., & Schuh, R. G. (1975). *Evaluation and educational decisionmaking: A functional guide to evaluating career education.* Washington, DC: Development Associates, for the Department of Health, Education, and Welfare.

The appendix of this booklet contains descriptions of nine instruments recommended by the authors and three "promising" instruments, all of which are relevant to career education either at the elementary or secondary level. Another instrument is described that receives mixed reviews.

Test descriptions include grade level, administration time, format, scoring, and cost. The book lists student outcomes relevant to career education and uses a table to match these with recommended or promising tests.

Lehman, P. R. (1968). *Tests and measurements in music.* Englewood Cliffs, NJ: Prentice-Hall.

This book contains descriptions and evaluations of published tests of music achievement and auditory and musical aptitudes as well as advice about constructing your own tests, and a discussion of measurement problems involved in measuring music appreciation and instrument performance. The author describes and evaluates 10 published tests in the aptitude category, 13 in the achievement category, and 1 test of band instrument performance.

The appendix suggests further readings relevant to measuring musical achievement. Some deal with use and adaptation of commercially published music tests; others consist of journal articles containing tests that, according to the author, are well known but were never commercially published.

In addition, major test publishers provide catalogs of instruments available for purchase. Publishers you can contact include the Riverside Publishing Company, Chicago, Illinois; Psychological Corporation, Cleveland, Ohio; Charles E. Merrill Publishing Company: Test Division, Columbus, Ohio; and CTB/McGraw-Hill, Monterey, California.

The following sources might contain tests of interest to you as well (the contents of publications marked with an asterisk are described in Chapter 4):

American Alliance for Health, Physical Education, and Recreation. (1976). *Testing for impaired, disabled, and handicapped individuals.*＊ Washington: Author.

American Association for Vocational Instructional Materials. (1976). *Vocational competency measures project.* Athens, GA: Author.

Beck, D., & Beck, H. (1981). *Evaluating classroom speaking.* Annandale, VA: Speech Communication Association.

Fagan, W. T., Cooper, C. R., & Jensen, J. M. (1975). *Measures for research and evaluation in the English language arts.*＊ Urbana, IL: ERIC Clearinghouse on Reading and Communication Skills and National Council of Teachers of English.

Hunsicker, P., & Reiff, G. G. (1975) *Youth fitness test manual.*＊ Washington, DC: American Alliance for Health, Physical Education, and Recreation.

Johnson, B. L., & Nelson, J. K. (1974). *Practical measurements for evaluation in physical education.*＊ Minneapolis, MN: Burgess.

Mayer, V. J. (1974). *Unpublished instruments in science education: A handbook.*＊ Columbus: ERIC/SMEAC Reference Center, Ohio State

```
┌────────────────────────────────────────────────────────────────────┐
│ Copper Falls County School System                                  │
│ 1400 Minocqua Drive                     PURCHASE ORDER NUMBER       │
│ Ironwood. Michigan 49938                                           │
│ (412) 772-0047                             № 128                   │
├────────────────────────────────────────────────────────────────────┤
```

| TO: _____ | FROM: | Marianne Howard |
| | | Title XIV Coordinator |

DATE ORDERED	DATE NEEDED	SHIP VIA	SPECIAL INSTRUCTIONS
3-9-XX	4-15-XX	Post	

QUANTITY	DESCRIPTION	UNIT PRICE	AMOUNT
80	XYZ Reading Comprehension Test copies, Form ABC (CC 459)	.20	$16.00
100	XYZ Reading Comprehension Test answer sheets, Form ABC (CC 601)	.05	5.00
1	XYZ Reading Comprehension Test manual (CC 518)	.50	.50
2	XYZ Reading Comprehension Test scoring keys, Form ABC	.50	1.00

Figure 2. Sample purchase order

University, College of Education.

National Technical Information Service. (1983). *Evaluating the impact of training: A collection of federal agency evaluation practices.* Springfield, VA: Author.

Peace, B. A. (1965). Appendix: Bibliography of social studies tests. In National Council for the Social Studies, *Thirty-fifth yearbook: Evaluation in social studies* (pp. 230-238).* Washington, DC: National Council for the Social Studies.

Rubin, D., & Mead, N. (1984). *Large-scale assessment of oral communication skills: Kindergarten through grade 12.* Annandale, VA: Speech Communication Association.

Suydam, M. N. (1974). *Unpublished instruments for evaluation in mathematics education: An annotated listing.** Columbus, OH: ERIC Information Analysis Center for Science, Mathematics and Environmental Education.

Valette, R. M. (1977). Appendix: Commercial language tests. In *Modern language testing.** New York: Harcourt Brace Jovanovich.

Selecting and Ordering a Test

Chapter 3 provides a detailed, highly prescriptive procedure for determining how well a test suits your particular program. You may decide on other, less formal ways of making your selection.

In any case, once you have chosen a performance measure, the next step, of course, is to order it from the test publisher. Figure 2 shows a sample purchase order. The March 9 date on the purchase order was chosen for a reason. March is not too early in the year to order tests for May. You should allow at least two months for delivery so that you will have time in which to correct possible shipping errors. In addition, you should always give the publisher a shipping deadline that is well in advance of when you *must* have the test.

Notes

1. Issues of design are discussed in several useful texts. See, for instance Fitz-Gibbon and Morris (1987b) and Campbell and Stanley (1966).

2. Why does summing the decimals give you the average *raw* score? Because calculating the raw score from percents correct per item demands first dividing the sum of the percentages by the number of items to get the average percentage correct, and then multiplying again by this number to convert the average percentage correct to a raw score. The operations of dividing and then multiplying by the same number cancel each other.

Consider this example. A test has *five* items. Percentage of the participants getting each item correct is as follows:

Item	Percentage of Participants getting item correct	Translated Item to decimals
1	80%	.80
2	25%	.25
3	35%	.35
4	90%	.90
5	40%	.40
	2.70	= sum of decimals

.54   = mean percent
                correct over
                five items

To determine the average raw score from the five items, you must multiply .54 by 5. You get 2.70 again.

Chapter 3
Determining How Well a Test Fits the Program

Before you select a performance test, you should find out all you can about its development, procedures for administration, technical quality, and, if possible, the success of its previous use. If you are able to find an evaluation of the particular measure in the educational literature, you will have a good start toward test selection. If not, you will have to depend on the information provided by the publisher. Request a specimen set well before you will need the test—three or four months in advance. When sample measures arrive, look them over with a critical eye.

The test you use for assessing the performance outcomes of a program should be the one that allows you most confidently to make this statement: *There is a close fit between the items or tasks constituting the test and the major objectives of the program being evaluated.* The major criterion for test selection is relevance.

Determining relevance will require a *close examination of the items or tasks and procedures included on the test.* This chapter is intended to help you examine tests for their appropriateness to your program evaluation.

A word should be said, however, about the *timing* of the evaluation and your own potential influence on the shape of the program. The procedures described in this chapter assume that the objectives of the program are *fixed* and that the program was already underway when the evaluation began. This will almost certainly be the case if you are a summative evaluator and will characterize many formative situations as well. If you are in the fortunate position of starting the evaluation *before* the program has begun, though, you might be able to influence program content. If, during planning or initial implementation you were to locate a test closely related to the program and well suited to the participants in question, then you could try to persuade planners *to develop the program with the test in mind.* This would assure you *in advance* that the program addressed the objectives of the test. Of course, the desirability of basing objectives on a test is a controversial issue. Some educators who lean toward humanism, for instance, deplore this as teaching to the test; and it is conceivable that such a practice, if improperly carried out, might narrow the curriculum or program to an overemphasis on piecemeal skills. The suggestion, however, is not that objectives from the test form the sole basis for the curriculum. They should simply be included in curriculum planning. It is unfair, after all, to expect participants to perform well on a test whose objectives have not been addressed by their instruction, particularly if this test is one on which good scores are expected by the audience that the program serves.

A Procedure for Locating an Appropriate Test

If the content of the program has already been established, you have the option of selecting or constructing a test. The next chapter details the basic steps to be followed if you intend to construct a test for program evaluation. This chapter contains a three-step process for judging test appropriateness that is designed to help you select the most relevant test. The steps in this process are outlined in Table 4.

Step 3, the last step in the process, describes how to use the *Table for Program Test Comparison* (TPTC) to arrive at numerical values—a Grand Average, Indices of Coverage and Relevance, and Number of Items per Objective. These tell you how well particular tests match the program's most important objectives. The TPTC (shown here as Table 6) has been adapted from a procedure suggested by the Center for the Study of Evaluation in *The CSE Test Evaluation Series.*[1]

Although the procedure for determining test-program match outlined here is highly detailed and prescriptive, you might attend to the rationale on which it is based without following the procedure to the letter.

Step 1. Refine and Classify Objectives

Obtain the best description you can find of the program's performance goals and objectives, or derive them from an outline of the curriculum or other components covered by the program. Then revise these statements in consultation with the program staff until you have an agreed-upon list of significant program objectives. This list plays an important role in the test selection procedure, so make sure that it describes as specifically as possible what the program intends to achieve. The most helpful

TABLE 4
Outline of Steps for Determining How Well a Test Matches Your Program

Step 1. Refine and Classify Objectives*

A. Obtain a list of program objectives or an outline of curriculum topics and make sure they are stated as specifically as possible..

B. Then classify program objectives and select as many of them as you will be able to test. You may use one or more of the following methods:

1. Take a random sample if there are many objectives of about equal importance.

2. Have interested people from your audience rate or rank-order objectives. This increases the probability that the test or tests selected for the evaluation will be fair to the interests of the program's *constituency*. This is primarily a summative evaluation concern.

3. Have someone who knows the program's subject area organize program objectives into a skills hierarchy, and use it to help you decide which objectives it is most important to test. The objectives that should be emphasized in test selection are the more complex skills toward which the program builds, in the case of summative evaluation; whereas more attention to key enroute or component skills is needed for selection of tests for formative evaluation.

4. Have someone who knows the program sort objectives according to how closely they match the program *as implemented*.

Step 2. Obtain and Screen Test Specimens

A. Review the educational literature for critiques of relevant tests.

B. Obtain sample measures from publishers.

C. Screen the tests according to criteria you have decided upon.

D. Retain for consideration tests which meet the standards of the evaluation.

Step 3. For Each Test Under Consideration, Estimate the Relative Match of the Test Items to the Program Objectives from Step 1

A. Using the Table for Program-Test Comparison, number or code all test items and record these in column 1.

B. Number or code each program objective.

C. In column 2, record for each test item the program objective(s) addressed.

D. In column 3, record a value that reflects the importance of the objective.

E. In column 4, record a value (0, 1, or 2) for closeness of item content and format to the objective.

F. In column 5, record a value (0, 1, or 2) to reflect item appropriateness for the examinees.

G. In column 6 and 7 calculate the following:

• The product of the values in columns 3, 4, and 5.

• A Grand Average (sum of column 6 products ÷ number of items in column 1).

• Index of Coverage (total number of different objectives in column 2 ÷ total number of objectives).

• Index of Relevance (total number of non-zero products in column 6 ÷ total number of items in column 1).

---

*It is possible to choose a test according to its fit with the program *without* looking at explicit program objectives. Such a procedure, which is described on page 65, requires that people intimately familiar with the program perform a modified version of Step 3 only. This amounts to comparing tests by matching them to *implicit* program objectives.

statement of an objective is one that depicts what a test item for that objective might look like. If you will be working from a curriculum outline, look through the instructional materials themselves to further clarify vaguely stated topics in the outline. Sometimes statements of objectives will accompany published materials. Unfortunately, some publishers do a poor job of writing objectives to go with their materials, so you may find only a loose relationship between the objectives for which the materials are designed and the test's activities. In that case, the publisher's objectives will be of little or no value to you.

Once you have a complete set of program objectives, you probably will want to shorten the list. In using the TPTC to compare the relevance of educational tests, 30 to 50 objectives is a manageable number. Depending on the rating method you use, you might be able to reduce the size of the set of objectives and rate them at the same time.

Reducing the Set and Rating Objectives for Importance[2]

The procedures for reducing the size of a set of objectives outlined in this section were briefly described in Table 3 (page 27). You may want to check Table 3 for a review of the advantages and disadvantages of each method. It is also possible to use some combination of these methods.

Take a random sample

The quickest way to narrow down the number of objectives is to choose some at random from the larger pool. If the selection of a test used for the evaluation will be based upon a random sample of objectives, then *all* objectives have been treated as being of equal importance, since the items from any objective could appear on the test. If program staff do not know at the outset of the program which of the program objectives will be tested, they are less likely to narrow the focus of the program to only those objectives that will be measured.

Simple random sampling, however, might expose your test results to the criticism, "You didn't test for the most important skill we wanted the participants to learn." You can avoid this situation by having members of your evaluation audience or the staff add to the random sample a few more of what they consider to be the *more critical* objectives.

Have interested members of your audience rate objectives

Rating of objectives by members of the program's constituency assists you in choosing a test that reflects the objectives most important to the people who want an assessment of the program. Such a procedure, which could be called a *retrospective needs assessment*,[3] is particularly useful for summative evaluation.

If you decide to ask people to rate objectives, choose a set of raters who represent the viewpoints of the program's constituency. The number of raters is up to you. Ask the raters to examine the pool of objectives and then sort them into categories with point values:

1 points	Unimportant
2 points	Below average importance
3 points	Average importance
4 points	Above average importance
5 points	Very important, critical, or essential

Instruct the raters to base their decisions on what *they* think the participants should learn from the program. Collect the ratings or rankings and compute a mean per objective for the whole set of raters. If raters' opinions tend to polarize, you will have to calculate mean ratings to represent the views of the different interest groups. The 30 to 50 highest ranking objectives (or whatever number you are prepared to test) would then be used as the basis for choosing the test.

Have someone who knows the subject area or the program rationale construct a skills hierarchy

A hierarchy reflects the order in which skills are presumably learned. A test based on objectives rated in this way will contain a greater proportion of items that measure achievement of the "terminal" objectives toward which the program builds, and fewer of the "en route" skills whose presence can be inferred from mastery of the more advanced objectives.

Usually hierarchies are constructed by first sorting objectives into three categories: simple, intermediate, and complex or terminal performance objectives. Then graphs, like the one in Figure 3, are constructed, showing interrelationships—that is, which objectives must be mastered in order to learn the others. Highest priority is usually given to those objectives that represent ultimate program goals and to those objectives, such as objective 1 in Figure 3, that feed into more than one subsequent objective.

Have someone who knows the program sort objectives according to how closely they match the program as implemented

The best test on which to base decisions about modifications in a program is one that measures the effectiveness of what the program is

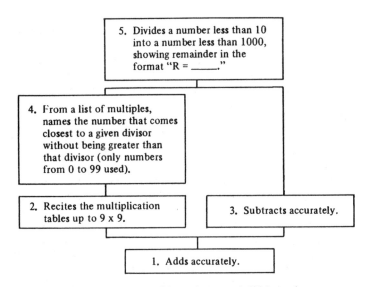

Figure 3. Portion of long division skill hierarchy

actually trying hardest to do. A test reflecting the objectives of the program as implemented is indispensable for formative evaluation. For summative evaluation, such a test is a fair basis for judgment of program effectiveness. It holds the staff accountable for accomplishing what they actually attempted.

In order to rate objectives according to the extent to which they reflect the program in operation, you will need one or two people who have seen the program in action and have carefully examined the curriculum. Have them classify objectives into four categories:

Official-Implemented Objectives. Objectives that are listed in the program proposal, plan, or curriculum outline, and that have received considerable attention as the program takes place at *nearly all its sites* should be given highest priority when a test is selected. These are important to everyone.

Official-Not Implemented Objectives. Objectives that were announced but that the program did not address should *not* be reflected in the test. They may have been originally included to make the program more appealing to the funding source or to round out a portrayal of the program's comprehensiveness. More often than not, neglected objectives are a sign that the ambitions of program planners simply exceeded what staff could realistically be expected to carry out.

Transfer and Generalization Objectives. These are stated objectives that fit into neither of the first two categories. They are typically generalization and transfer skills that participants in the program *might* develop in connection with their interaction in the program but that are not expressly addressed by the program activities. It would be unfair to hold the program accountable for the attainment of these objectives since they are peripheral to the program's focus. Test selection should lean a little toward these objectives, but not too far.

Unofficial-Implemented Objectives. It is possible that the program as implemented—*at least at some of its sites*—strives toward objectives that have not been mentioned in official documents and that do not appear in your original list. Request that whoever classified the objectives take some time to search out performance ambitions of the program staff that have gone unrecorded. A program may have acquired these additional objectives in any number of ways. Some might represent prerequisite skills that were added because of deficiencies in the skills or knowledge of entering participants. Others probably just evolved, whether because of participant interests, staff judgments, or special opportunities for learning that arose during the program. Whatever the reason for their appearance, the program gives them some attention, so they should also be part of what the test measures.

Classifying objectives—by ratings, hierarchies, or degree of implementation—gives you information that can help you to select tests. Not only can you make a general judgment about the test's appropriateness to the program objectives, you can also select different tests on the basis of which *kind* of objectives they address. In addition, your classification can be useful to you when all the data are in and you must interpret test results for your report.

Classifying objectives can also be an important way of involving as many interested people as you can in the evaluation process. You should, of course, report back to them the resulting classification as a picture of your perception of the program's goals. If you are a formative evaluator, such information should be flowing back and forth anyway. If you are a summative evaluator, this communication can help you and your audience to arrive at a common understanding of the program's aims. Such conversations contribute to the credibility of the evaluation.

Step 2. Obtain and Screen Test Specimens

Completing the Table for Program-Test Comparison (TPTC) requires effort. You will therefore want to limit this rigorous examination to the few tests that you are considering seriously. Before you sit down with the table, therefore, you should *screen* the test specimens you have located.

Your *criteria* for screening tests will depend on your situation. They will reflect the demands you or your audience intend to make of the test concerning, for instance, types of scores provided, test length, or technical quality. To examine your thinking about major test features, complete the short questionnaire in Table 5. Then eliminate tests that omit the features that are most important to you.

Step 3. For Each Test Under Consideration, Estimate the Relative Match of the Test Items to the Program Objectives in Step 1

Table 6, the Table for Program-Test Comparison (TPTC), is designed to help you perform a detailed analysis of the relevance of a test for systematically measuring the outcomes of the program. Using the TPTC involves one-by-one comparison of each of the test's items with the most important objectives of the program being evaluated. The method has several advantages over informal assessments of this match:

(1) It is systematic. The procedure can be explained to people, used over and over with different tests, and modified to suit your situation.

(2) The step-by-step procedure calls attention to characteristics of a test that should determine test selection in any situation. It helps you to compute separately the following:

- the *Grand Average*—a general index of the relative appropriateness of the test for measuring the program's highest priority objectives with your particular target group of participants. A high Grand Average means that the test contains a large proportion of items addressed to the program's most important objectives;
- the proportion of items on the test that are relevant to the program— the *Index of Relevance*;
- the proportion of the objectives of the program covered by the test— the *Index of Coverage*;
- the number of test items per program objective.

(3) Because there are so many judgments to make, the procedure uses *numerical ratings* to represent test characteristics. This enables you to aggregate judgments into the indices just described. The indices then give you an easy method for comparing tests.

For your convenience, Appendix A contains a larger Table for Program-Test Comparison that can be photocopied. A step-by-step description of how to fill in the table begins on this page and continues through page 65.

TABLE 5
Test Selector's Screening Questionnaire

Feature	Importance Rating				
	barely		moderately		crucially
1. The grade or proficiency levels for which the test is intenced	1	2	3	4	5
2. Whether sex, cultural, ethnic and geographic bias have been minimized	1	2	3	4	5
3. How long the test or selected subtests take to administer	1	2	3	4	5
4. Whether the test has undergone field tryouts	1	2	3	4	5
5. The sorts of scores provided -- raw scores only, percentiles, stanines, mastery cut-offs per objective	1	2	3	4	5
6. Whether the test items* are explicitly keyed to specific skills or objectives	1	2	3	4	5
7. How precisely test objectives or skills have been described	1	2	3	4	5
8. Whether there is more than one item for each objective measured	1	2	3	4	5
9. Whether the subjects in the field test and norm sample are a national cross-section	1	2	3	4	5
10. Whether the subjects in the field test and norm sample are comparable to your participants	1	2	3	4	5
11. Whether the written materials and instructions are appropriate both in terms of clarity and appeal, for the participants in your program	1	2	3	4	5
12. Whether the test has alternate forms	1	2	3	4	5
13. Clarity of the instructions to the examiner	1	2	3	4	5

(continued)

TABLE 5 (continued)
Test Selector's Screening Questionnaire

Feature	Importance Rating				
	barely		moderately		crucially
14. Whether test items are indexed to various curricular materials for prescriptive purposes	1	2	3	4	5
15. Whether validity data are adequate and favorable	1	2	3	4	5
16. Whether reliability data are adequate and favorable	1	2	3	4	5
17. How well the test scores differentiate among low performers	1	2	3	4	5
18. How well the test scores differentiate among high performers	1	2	3	4	5
19. How credible and useful the instructions are on using scores for judging participants' mastery or non-mastery	1	2	3	4	5
20. How easy it is for participants to record their answers	1	2	3	4	5
21. The ease and objectivity of scoring	1	2	3	4	5
22. Whether a record keeping system is provided for use in individualized instruction	1	2	3	4	5

*Appendix B lists some more specific questions you might ask about item quality.

SOURCE: Adapted from Dotseth, Hunter, and Walker (1978).

How to Complete the Table for Program-Test Comparison (TPTC)

The TPTC has seven columns for recording the results of each step in the process of matching test items with program objectives. In column 1, you are asked to list the numbers of test items. Column 2 calls for you to find and note which of the program's objectives best matches each item.

Completing each remaining step requires that you *assign points* showing the importance or appropriateness of the items and objectives. Column 3 records your judgment of the *importance to the program of the objectives the item measures.* In column 4, you write down your judgment of the *appropriateness of the item's format and content* for measuring the objective. Column 5 records the item's appropriateness to the participants in question. Once columns 3 through 5 have been filled in, the numbers you have recorded are multiplied. Their product is noted in column 6. Data from these columns are then used to compute indices of coverage and relevance to help you to decide which test is best for measuring the particular objectives of the program.

Before you begin filling out the table, assemble specimens of the tests you plan to examine and a list of program objectives arranged according to their priority. *Be sure that each test item and written objective is numbered* or has been assigned some letter/number code that can be entered into columns 1 and 2.

Precisely *who* fills out the TPTC depends on circumstances. Armed with prioritized objectives, you can probably do a fairly effective job yourself. A good way to reduce the effects of rater errors and idiosyncrasies is for you to adjudicate the judgments of *two or three raters* or average the indices they obtain. People working with the TPTC should know the objectives practically by heart. They will need to remember relevant objectives when they read the test items.

Completing the TPTC requires following this step-by-step procedure:

Fill in identifying information

Supply relevant information at the top of the table—the test name and level, the subject matter area, the level of participants for whom the publisher says the test is most appropriate, whether the test is norm-(NRT) or criterion-referenced (CRT), the rater's name, and the date. In box A, fill in the total number of objectives used for test selection.

Column 1: List the test items

Since you will complete the table with the test in front of you, you need only enter in column 1 a numerical identifier for each test item. If the items on the test are numbered—simply 1 through, say, 50—then write these down. Otherwise, use a numerical or letter-number code of your own to distinctively identify items. If the test you are evaluating has quite a few items, you will have to have several copies of the table.

Be sure when completing this step to list the test's *items*, not its

TABLE 6
Table for Program-Test (TPTC)

Test_____   Subject area___ _____

Type: ☐ CRT ☐ NRT ☐ Unclear   Test level_____

                                    Participant level ___ _____

1 Test item	2 Objectives that match item	3 Importance of objective					4 Item content and format analysis		
		1	2	3	4	5	0	1	2

box B   Total # of items on the test

box C   # of *different* objectives listed

TABLE 6 (continued)
Table for Program-Test (TPTC)

Rated by _____

Date _____

| box A | Total # of program objectives used for selection |

5 Item appropriateness for participants			6 Product of columns 3, 4, and 5	7
				Summary figures
0	1	2		**Grand Average**
				Grand Tally (box D) ÷ total # of items on the test (box B) =
				Index of Coverage
				# of objectives listed in column 2 (box C) ÷ total # of program objectives (box A) =
				Index of Relevance
				# of products in column 6 (box E) ÷ total # of items on the test (box B) =

| box D | Grand Tally |

| box E | # of products in column 6 > 0 |

objectives—even if the test has been based on objectives that the publisher has provided. Test publishers often include statements of objectives with published tests—normed as well as criterion-referenced. The objectives often appear in the test's manual, and in some tests they are actually written on the test form. *If the test's items are available, it is inappropriate to use the announced objectives of the test as your indication of what the test measures.* It is the *items*, after all, that the examinees will encounter, regardless of the objectives written by the test publisher. And these items will be used to measure attainment of *the program's* objectives. The publisher's objectives need not enter into your decision about test appropriateness at all. For this reason, you would do well to either ignore the objectives that accompany the test, or use them as a basis for *initial* screening.

Now fill in columns 2 through 5 for each item, *working across the page rather than down the columns.* A straight edge or a ruler will help you keep your place.

Columns 2 and 3: Find the objective that best matches the item and record its importance rating

To complete column 2, match your list of objectives with each of the test items. Decide which program objective, if any, the item seems to measure, and write down the objective's number or code name. This task will be relatively easy if all the objectives are fresh in your memory and you understand them well. Then *double-check* the list of objectives to ensure that your matches make sense and to look for objectives you may have forgotten. Note that *the objective and item need not match exactly.* If you are in doubt about whether an item and/or objective match, decide that they *do.* The *degree of match* can be more precisely assessed later when you complete column 4. What is important here is to record the objectives that are addressed *at all* by the test, even peripherally.

It may occur to you that an item seems to assess *more than one* objective. You should list in column 2 *every* objective the item seems to address. But because completing columns 3, 4, and 5 with multiple objectives per item will be too complex, you will need to choose *one* of the objectives to use as a reference when filling in columns 3, 4, and 5. Which objective you choose is up to you, but you will probably want to select the one the item seems to assess most closely, and circle the entry for that objective.

While completing the TPTC you should notice that the test contains several similar items addressed to the same objective. In most cases, this is a desirable test feature. To avoid repeating test analysis every time a similar item occurs, simply copy across columns the information from the first occurrence of an item of a particular type.

Filling in column 2 equips you eventually to determine two other important characteristics of the test: the number of items referencing each objective, and the objectives that are and are not covered by the test. These are determined after the table has been completed.

If the item in column 1 seems to measure *no objective* of the program, then write "none" in column 2, and *draw a horizontal line all the way across the table to show that you need not consider that particular item again.* If you find that this exercise has eliminated more than a quarter of the test items from consideration, then think about declaring the test irrelevant to the program.

While you are completing column 2, also fill in column 3. The numerals entered into column 3 are *points* given each objective entered or circled in column 2 to reflect its relative importance.

Column 3 has space for assigning up to 5 points. You need not, however, use this wide a range. To complete column 3 write down the numbers of points assigned to the objective in the appropriate space, as in Figure 4.

How you complete column 3 depends on which method you use to select and prioritize objectives (pages 24 to 28). If you *sampled objectives* randomly, or if for any reason they have not been prioritized, then ignore column 3. If your sample contains some objectives of higher priority than the others, you could assign them 2 or 3 points by asking, Are they 2 or 3 times more important? Other objectives in the sample should receive 1 point.

If interested members of the program's constituency ranked or rated objectives, then enter in column 3 the average number of points assigned or the relative rank of the objective. As you will remember, a 5-point rating scale was suggested for this procedure.

If a *skills hierarchy* determined priority, points can be assigned objectives according to their relative importance for mastering the subject area. Since a 5-point range probably demands too fine a discrimination among objectives rated by this method, assign 1, 2, or 3 points. Give 3 points to terminal objectives toward which much of the curriculum builds, and to intermediate objectives that are prerequisite to a large number of other objectives. Give 2 points to other terminal objectives and less crucial intermediates, and 1 point to any other objectives.

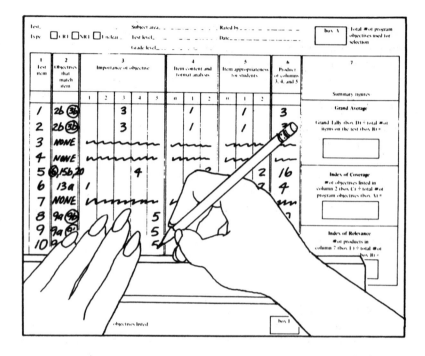

Figure 4. Filling in the Table for Program-Test Comparison (TPTC)

If objectives were classified according to the degree to which they underlie the program *as implemented*, then use a 3-point range: Assign Official and Unofficial-Implemented Objectives 3 points; give Transfer and Generalization Objectives 2 points; and Official-Not Implemented Objectives 1 point.

You could, as well, combine results from the different prioritizing procedures. How you assign points in column 3 and how many you assign are up to you—*as long as your procedure remains consistent throughout the whole test-program match exercise.*

The point values entered into column 3, you will note, *weight* the indices toward tests that contain items measuring the most important program objectives.

Using columns 4 and 5, you will examine the appropriateness of item content and format for measuring the objectives and for administration to the participant group in question. Items that receive high ratings in column 3 because they are associated with important objectives can be *promoted*, so to speak, if they again receive high ratings in columns 4 and 5 for *degree of match* with the objectives and participants. On the other hand, these items can be demoted if they receive low ratings.

Column 4: Match the content and format of item and objective

When completing column 2, you listed objectives from the program that seemed to be related to test items, disregarding somewhat the closeness of this relationship. Column 4 asks that you make a more precise decision about how closely the item and objective match. This decision is based on an analysis of the test item's *content and format*.

Content analysis means looking for overlap between the knowledge or performance required by the test and the program ambitions stated by the objective. This analysis is critical if you are to ensure finding a valid measure of the program's effectiveness. You can determine this overlap by asking yourself, for each item, the following sorts of questions:

- What specific *learning* does the item seem to measure? What specific math skills, for instance, or what grade level in reading? What kinds of topics are covered in the reading section: scientific, biographical, fiction? Is the *vocabulary* used in the test items similar to that used in the program?
- Is the item something the participant might actually have encountered during the course of the program? Are these the sorts of equations used in performing calculations? Does the unit on nutrition, for instance, mention this particular principle? Do the reading exercises cover this sort of subject matter?

Column 4 allows you to enter either a 0, a 1, or a 2. These point values represent a continuum of match between the item and the objective. A good strategy is to first classify the objective's *content*, giving it a tentative rating of 0, 1, or 2, before analyzing its format. Assume, first, that the content match between item and objective is so-so, and give the item a rating of 1. If the match seems particularly apt, then promote the rating to 2. If you have serious doubts about the appropriateness of the fit, and perhaps even about your decision in column 2 that the objectives matches the item at all, then assign a value of 0. If item content matches *no other* objective, then stop considering the item altogether.

After you have analyzed content, move on to a consideration of *format*. The critical question in examining a test for *appropriateness of format* is, *Do item formats on the test correspond to those that are learned by the participants in the program?* If the test is to be valid for your purposes, they should. A format that is new to participants might prevent them from demonstrating knowledge that they indeed have. Students, for example, who are accustomed to vertical presentations for adding fractions, for example,

$$
\begin{array}{r}
\frac{1}{2} \\
+ \frac{1}{4} \\
\hline
=
\end{array}
$$

might be confused by a problem on the test that is arranged $\frac{1}{2} + \frac{1}{4} =$ _____. Though they know how to add fractions, the format may trip them up. Too much format interference of this sort will invalidate the test.

It is quite likely that you will find *some* format differences between the presentation of items on the test and the experiences of participants in the program. *If you think that format differences will not seriously affect test results, then let the numeral you chose to represent the match between test content and program objectives represent your opinion.* Enter this quantity in column 4. On the other hand, if you think that format differences might seriously affect performance on this item, then reduce your rating of the match between the item and the objective accordingly, and record this numeral instead.

If you find that you have had to enter a zero in column 4 because of content or format mismatch, then draw a horizontal line through that row of the table. Entering a zero in any column will cause the eventual row product to equal zero.

In summary, a good strategy for arriving at a numerical value for column 4 is to assume first that the match between item and objective is so-so, allowing the rating to be 1. If you have doubts about the appropriateness of fit between either content or format, then reduce your rating to 0. On the other hand, if the item seems to fit the objective well, then increase your rating to 2.

Column 5: Rate the item's appropriateness for the program's target group

Even if the content and format of an item appear to match an important objective, it is still possible that the wording or amount of previous experience assumed by the item makes it inappropriate for the developmental level, ethnic background, or other quality of the group who are to be tested. Column 5 allows you to make a quick assessment of the item, assigning 0, 1, 2 points to denote appropriateness for the test takers. Appropriateness is often just a matter of whether the item is too easy or too hard for the group. Information in the test manual about difficulty indices per item might aid this decision. Again, a good strategy for completing column 5 is to first assume that the item is appropriate enough to deserve a rating of 1. If, however, the item seems just too easy or too hard, assign a rating of 0; if it is highly appropriate or just about perfect, promote the rating to 2.

Column 6: Combine judgments for each item

Multiply the numbers in columns 3, 4, and 5. Enter this product in column 6.

The test you are examining might be one that allows you to administer subtests of your own choosing and eliminate others. If this is the case, then *weed out* subtests whose absence will increase the test's relevance to the program *before* you go on to column 7 and calculate indices for test choice.

Column 7: Complete the summary figures and indices

Column 7 lists equations for calculating three indices for each test so that you can compare the appropriateness of different tests for measuring program objectives. These are the three indices:

(1) *The Grand Average.* This is computed by adding the products in column 6 to produce a Grand Tally, and then dividing the Grand Tally by the total number of test items listed in column 1. The Grand Average is the best summary index for deciding which of the tests you have analyzed is most appropriate to the program. *The test with the largest Grand Average covers your most important objectives most adequately.* Note, however, that this is a *relative* judgment: *Better than* the other tests does not mean *adequate.* A test with a high Grand Average might still leave important objectives unmeasured. The extent to which this has occurred can be estimated from the Index of Coverage.

You might also want to compare the Grand Average you have obtained with the maximum possible. If *all* the tests you examine score too low you might decide not to use any of them. The maximum Grand Average possible in each of your test analysis exercises will equal

the maximum number of points in
column 3 possible per objective $\times\,4$

The smallest value that the Grand Average can assume is, of course, zero.

(2) *An Index of Coverage.* Coverage—the extent to which the test *covers* program objectives—equals the proportion of program objectives measured by the test. To compute the index, first count the number of *different* objectives listed in column 2. *If some items were found to be relevant to two or more objectives, count all of them.* If a row of entries was crossed out because a zero rating occurred in columns 4 or 5, *do not* count the objective mentioned in that row. Enter the sum of the different objectives covered in box C below column 2; then divide this number by the total number of objectives on your initial list, the quantity in box A.

The maximum possible Index of Coverage is 1; the minimum, 0. In cases where the Index of Coverage is high, say, 75 or better, you can feel secure that the test represents the program fairly—particularly if the test ranks well according to other indices. If the index is low, then find out *which* objectives the test covers and omits. It probably concentrates on a certain *category* of skills, ignoring others. If this is so, then you know where the test is deficient, and you might be able to choose two tests that, combined, cover a larger set of program objectives. You could, as well, *construct* a test to measure the objectives left out and/or those that are poorly measured by the test you are thinking of selecting. You can get an idea of which objectives are measured poorly by looking at the fourth index, Number of Items per Objective, described below.

(3) *An Index of Relevance.* This index tells you what proportion *of the test* fits your set of objectives, and conversely, how much of the test is *irrelevant* to your evaluation. To compute the Index of Relevance, first count *the number of products* in column 6 that *do not equal zero* and enter this quantity in box E below that column. Then divide by the total number of items on the test. The Index of Relevance will have a value between 0 and 1; it tells you about what proportion of the time respondents taking the test will actually be working on tasks relevant to program objectives. The logical opposite of this measure, of course, is the proportion of time respondents will spend displaying skills that have nothing to do with program instruction.

In addition to the three indices in column 7, the TPTC allows you to compute a set of values that will be important if you intend to interpret test results objective-by-objective: the *Number of Items per Objective.* You can determine this by looking at column 2, and counting how many times each particular objective is mentioned. The reliability of a test is strongly related to the number of items the test contains. A reliable test of a single objective should contain at least three, and ideally five, items. If you notice that only one or two items cover each objective, the test might still allow you to make *summary statements about the program in general*; but you will be unable to say anything about the performance of individuals on any *particular* objective.

How to Use the Table for Program-Test Comparison Without Program Objectives

In the absence of clearly written objectives, you can adapt the TPTC procedure and choose a test based on how well the program's *staff* feels the test fits the *program*. This amounts to asking people who know the program well to evaluate the test according to their implicit notions of the program's aims. To do this, augment the standard procedure in the following way:

- List test items in column 1 of the TPTC as the test selection procedure recommends, and cross out column 2.
- Give the candidate tests and the TPTC to a few people who are intimate with the program, and have them begin test examination at column 3. Ask the staff members to assign a 1-to-5 rating on each item according to the importance of the skill it measures to the overall program.
- Have the raters complete columns 4, 5, and 6 as prescribed.
- In column 7, compute the Grand Average and Index of Relevance. Because you are without a pool of explicit objectives, you will be unable to compute an Index of Coverage. You will *not* be able to count the number of test items per objective, the fourth index of interest.
- Have the group of raters give you an informal Index of Coverage by estimating the proportion of the program the test does seem to cover and by listing program areas it fails to touch on at all.

Then choose a test

In many cases, the test most useful for your evaluation will be the one with the largest Grand Average, particularly if this average is close to the maximum possible. It will come closest to measuring the program's most important objectives. Be careful, however, to temper your choice based on the Grand Average with a look at the other indices.

Regardless of the size of the Grand Average, you probably should not use a test that has an Index of Coverage lower than about .65, unless you can test in some other way for attainment of the objectives the test omits.

On the other hand, a test with a very high Grand Average and a low Index of Coverage probably omits mainly lower priority objectives. In this case, you may decide to just ignore those objectives. A test with a comparatively high Grand Average will rarely show a low Index of Relevance. If this does happen, it means that a small part of the test is doing a good job of measuring some important program objectives. The Grand Average has been inflated by their high ratings in column 3. Unless you will be able to extract and administer only those items that are relevant to the program, such a test is probably not suitable for evaluating it.

The Number of Items per Objective is an important index to consider *if you intend to interpret the test's results objective-by-objective*. In general, you will be able to announce with confidence that participants have attained particular objectives only if the test contains four or five items per objective. What is more, when you interpret the results for each objective, the items should be fairly homogeneous and close to the objectives in content and format (the concern of column 4). Regardless of other indices, a test that allots each objective only 1, 2, or 3 items may not give you a reliable indication of their attainment.

On the other hand, if you plan to use the score from the whole test to reflect general program performance, then the Number of Items per Objective will carry less weight in influencing your choice. In this case, you should use your information about which objectives are addressed by which proportion of test items to assure that the test as a whole gives strong emphasis to important objectives and minor emphasis to less important ones. This is the issue of content validity, described on pages 98 to 103.

Notes

1. The procedure, formulated by L. Weinberger, appears in *CSE criterion-referenced test handbook*, produced by C. B. Walker et al. (1979).

2. Step-by-step guidance in sampling objectives and rating according to audience preferences and objectives hierarchies is contained in Morris, L.L. & Fitz-Gibbon, C.T., "How to deal with goals and objectives," in L. L. Morris (1978) (ed.) *Program evaluation kit*. Newbury Park, CA: Sage.

3. A needs assessment is a commonly used method for gathering opinion about priorities placed on objectives.

For Further Reading

American Psychological Association, American Educational Research Association, and National Council on Measurement in Education. (1974). *Standards for educational and psychological tests and manuals.* Washington, DC: American Psychological Association.

Armbruster, B. B., Stevens, R. J., & Rosenshire, B. (1977). Analyzing content coverage and emphasis: A study of three curricula and two tests. *Technical Report No. 26.* Urbana: Center for the Study of Reading, University of Illinois.

Hambleton, R. K., & Eignor, D. (1978). Guidelines for evaluating criterion-referenced tests and test manuals. *Journal of Educational Measurement, 15,*(2).

Joint Committee on Standards for Educational Evaluation. (1980). *Standards for evaluation of educational programs, projects and materials.* New York: McGraw-Hill.

Jolly, S. J., & Glamenz, G. W. (1984). Customizing a norm-referenced achievement test to achieve curricular validity: A case study. *Educational Measurement: Issues and Practices, 3.*

Katz, M. (1973). *Selecting an achievement test.* Princeton, NJ: Educational Testing Service.

On the Topic of Sampling

Fitz-Gibbon, C. T., & Morris, L. L. (1987). *How to design a program evaluation* (2nd ed., chap. 8). Newbury Park, CA: Sage.

Chapter 4
Constructing a Test for Program Evaluation

There may be times when you decide to construct a performance test yourself, rather than use an existing measure, in order to have an instrument that better matches the particular program you are evaluating. Or the occasion may arise when you are conducting a large-scale evaluation and have the resources necessary to hire an external consultant or agency to custom design performance tests for the evaluation. In either case, you will want to be familiar with the basics of test construction so that you can successfully carry out or oversee the effort. This chapter is designed to help you learn those basics. The first part of the chapter walks you through the steps typically followed in developing a test. The second part lists a variety of resources that provide more in-depth explanations of how to construct high quality performance tests.

Basic Steps in Developing a Performance Test
for Program Evaluation

The development of a performance test can be summarized in five major steps. Those steps are listed below and described in the pages that follow.

(1) Determine the outcomes to be measured.
(2) Develop a blueprint for the test.
(3) Write the test items.
(4) Review and edit the items.
(5) Field test the items.
(6) Obtain reliability and validity data.

Step 1: Determine the outcomes to be measured

The development of any test begins with the selection of the outcomes that will be assessed. How to determine the outcomes to be used to guide the construction of a performance measure has already been discussed on pages 21 through 31 of Chapter 1. When you complete the procedures outlined there, you should have a list of the program objectives or outcomes that you wish to measure.

At this point, it is necessary to review the list of outcomes to make sure that each one is broad enough to support the development of five or more test items or test tasks to measure its attainment. If you have many very discrete objectives, each one of which equals a single test item only, you would be well advised to combine as many as possible into specific, but broader-scale, outcomes. Once this consolidation process is completed, you are ready to proceed to step 2.

Step 2: Develop a blueprint for the test

As with any construction task, you need a blueprint to guide your efforts. And as with most buildings, the more detailed the plans, the better the edifice.

If you are planning to develop a norm-referenced test, a content/process matrix such as the one shown in Table 1 on page 17 will be the sort of document that you will develop. The purpose of this matrix is to define, at only a very general level, the types of skills and content to be contained in the test items. Item writers will then use this matrix to develop a wide variety of test questions for each cell.

If you are planning to develop a criterion-referenced test, you need to develop a test blueprint that is far more specific. You must describe the skill being measured, the nature of the question or of the situation to which examinees are to respond, and the key dimensions of correct and incorrect responses in sufficient detail that a pool of essentially homogeneous test items or assessment tasks can be written. The test blueprint (sometimes called test specifications) becomes the criterion against which examinee performance can be evaluated.

In order to give you an idea of the level of specificity often found in the blueprint for a criterion-referenced test, an illustrative set of test specifications appears below. These specifications were developed to measure a performance outcome associated with a high school minimum competency program. The competency (or outcome) itself is stated at the beginning of the document, followed by a summary description of the test, a sample item, and the rules to be followed in developing the test items and answer choices. While this specification as well as commonly used tests call for a traditional paper-and-pencil measure requiring a selected response, recall your many options for assessment, including constructed response, essay-type items, simulations, work or other behavioral samples, ratings, observations and self-report.

Illustrative Test Specifications

READING TO LOCATE IDEAS

Competency Description

The ability to comprehend the main idea and supporting details in content such as newspaper and magazine articles, selections from textbooks, fictional selections, and business letters.

Test Description

The student will be presented with a selection from a newspaper or magazine article, a selection from a textbook, a fictional selection, or a business letter. Four statements will follow the selection. The student will select the one statement that presents the main idea of the selection at a literal level of comprehension.

Sample Item

Directions:

(1) Read the selections that follow.
(2) Choose the best main idea statement for each selection.
(3) Mark the letter of your choice on your answer sheet.

A WAY TO CHANGE YOUR HABITS

It is possible to stop your bad habits simply by using a rubber band. Here's how you do it. Wear a loose-fitting rubber band on one wrist. Whenever you practice a bad habit, stretch the rubber band and deliver a healthy snap to the the underside of your wrist. The very brief sting is like a shock. It is very important that you wear the rubber band at all times and that you give yourself the shock every time you practice a bad habit.

This method of stopping bad habits was started at the Penndel Center in Washington. In order to stop bad habits, people were given a battery-powered shock box. They were told to give themselves a shock whenever they practiced certain habits. This helped them to stop their bad habits. Doctors at the center then tried substituting a rubber band for the shock box. The doctors reported excellent results.

(1) Which one of the following sentences is the best statement of the main idea of the selection you just read?

    (a) People can stop their bad habits by using rubber bands.

    (b) Doctors help people stop bad habits.

    (c) A rubber band delivers a sting that is like a shock.

    (d) Doctors report that rubber bands are not helpful in stopping bad habits.

Question Description

(1) Each item will consist of a reading selection followed by the question, "Which one of the following sentences is the best statement of the main idea of the selection you just read?"

(2) Reading selections will be based on actual news and feature articles from newspapers and magazines, on actual selections from student textbooks, on fictional selections likely to be of interest to high school students, and on business letters appropriate to the experience level of the students being tested.

(3) Care will be taken to choose reading selections of interest to high school students and to avoid selections that may, presently or in the near future, appear dated. Controversial or overly stimulating topics will be avoided.

(4) Each reading selection will contain a main idea that is directly stated. This main idea need not appear in the opening sentence.

(5) All reading selections except business letters will be titled. Business letters will be presented in standard letter format. All selections will be at least one paragraph long, and will contain from 100 to 250 words. Selections will be kept as short as possible.

(6) In any set of five items, not more than 1,000 words of reading material will be tested.

(7) At least two of the five items in any set will contain selections that are more than one paragraph long.

(8) If necessary the following adaptations may be made to a selection's content:

    (a) A title will be added if the selection needs one but does not have one or if the selection represents a section of a longer piece whose title would not be applicable to the excerpt. The title should be composed of a brief, interest-getting and/or summarizing group of words. The title should not restate the main idea of the passage.

    (b) A selection may shortened, but only if the segment that is to be used for testing makes sense and stands as a complete unit of thought.

    (c) Minor editing, to increase clarity and continuity, may be done to a reading selection that represents a shortening of a longer piece.

    (d) Paragraphs will be indented or, in the case of business letters, presented in standard letter format.

(9) Reading selections used for testing should not exceed a secondary reading level, as judged by the Fry Readability Formula. Idioms will be avoided whenever possible.

Response Description

(1) Four single-sentence response options will follow each reading selection. Three will be incorrect responses and one will be the correct response. The statements will plausibly relate to the content of the reading selection, either by reiterating or paraphrasing portions of that selection, or by building upon a word or idea contained in the selection. A response option will not state an idea that is incapable of verification within the selection presented.

(2) A correct main idea statement will be characterized by two essential attributes: *accuracy* and *appropriate scope*.

    (a) A correct main idea statement must be accurate in that everything it states can be verified in the text that it describes.

    (b) A correct main idea statement must have appropriate scope in that it encompasses all of the most important points discussed in the text that it describes.

(3) Incorrect response options will be characterized by either a *lack of accuracy* or a *lack of appropriate scope*.

(4) An incorrect response exemplifies a *lack of accuracy* when it makes a statement contradicted by information in the text.

(5) An incorrect response exemplifies a *lack of appropriate scope* when it does one of two things:

    (a) Makes a statement that is too narrow in its scope and does not account for all of the important details contained in the text.

    (b) Makes a statement that is *significantly* too broad in its scope and is much more general than it needs to be in order to account for all of the important details contained in the text.

(6) The incorrect responses for any one item must include at least one statement that lacks accuracy and one statement that lacks appropriate scope.

(7) The important points that must be included in a main idea statement are those details that are emphasized in the text by structural, semantic, and rhetorical means (e.g., placement in a position of emphasis, repetition, synonymous rephrasing, elaboration). Whether any given main idea statement contains all of the important points in the text is

always debatable rather than indisputable. The nature of the question asked on this test (i.e., to select the *best* main idea statement from among those given) attempts to account for this quality of relative rather than absolute correctness. The correct response will be distinct enough from the incorrect responses to ensure a minimum of debate as to its relative correctness.

(8) The correct response will be either paraphrased or reiterated from the selection. It will be that statement that is both entirely accurate and of the most appropriate scope in relation to the other statements given.

(9) In any given set of items, 40% of the correct responses will be reiterated and 60% of the correct responses will be paraphrased from the selection.

(10) In constructing a set of response options for a single item, care will be taken to ensure that the correct response cannot be deduced by a process of elimination.

Step 3: Write the test items

As soon as the test is blueprinted, you are ready to begin development of the test items, following the rules stipulated in that blueprint. At this point you should also review a checklist such as the one presented in Appendix B, so that you avoid making common item construction errors. The total number of test items that you need to write depends upon the number of test items you plan to use in measuring the outcome as well as the number of equivalent test forms you hope to develop. You are always well advised to write substantially more items than you will ultimately need, as the review and field testing procedures that follow may eliminate some items from use.

Step 4: Review and edit the items

After the test items are written, they should be subjected to judgmental reviews as well as the critical eye of a good editor. Reviewers need to examine the items for congruence with the test blueprint, plausibility of answer choices, readability factors, and general overall quality. They should also be attentive to any potentially biasing elements in the items; that is, anything that could potentially advantage or disadvantage any subgroup of examinees within the population. The items should be revised based upon the results of the judgmental and editorial reviews.

Step 5: Field test the items or tasks

In order to verify that the test items are an appropriate measure of the skill being measured, they must be tried out with sample respondents so that empirical information about their performance can be collected and analyzed. The extent and rigor of the field test will depend upon the resources you have available as well as the stakes associated with the evaluation. If you are developing a performance test for the formative evaluation of a small-scale program, you can get away with fewer respondents and less sophisticated item analysis procedures. At a minimum, you would want to determine the difficulty level of each item (that is, the proportion of respondents who answer a question correctly) and the pattern of responses (that is, how many respondents are selecting each answer choice if it is a selected response type item or typical answers if it is a constructed response type item). If you are developing a high-stakes performance test, however, you will want to use more powerful analytic techniques and perhaps even work with a specialist in such procedures. Nowadays, for example, item response theory is one widely used method of item analysis. Consult the references cited at the end of this chapter for further information about this and other item analysis methodologies.

Step 6: Obtain reliability and validity data

Once you have field tested the items, selected those that performed well, and formatted the items into a completed instrument, you are ready to collect information on the reliability and validity of the measure. Since Chapter 5 deals with those issues in detail, they will not be described here. Suffice it to say, however, that you will need to marshal some sort of reliability and validity evidence in order to prove the worth of the measure you have created.

Available Resources

Even if you decide to construct your own performance test, suited to the particulars of the program you are evaluating, it is important to take advantage of the experience of others. You should try to become familiar with the dos and don'ts accumulated by professionals who have designed tests over the years. When you choose which objectives to measure and what types of items to use, you should know something about the alternatives you have rejected so that you can justify your measurement plan.

An abundance of advice is available to you in books and journals on the topics of constructing tests and describing student achievement. This part of the chapter lists a variety of existing resources to help you build a good test. Since *what is being measured* affects test construction and interpretation, Section 1 points out guides for assessing achievement in specific subjects. The section is divided into subject areas: the arts, career and vocational education, English/language arts, foreign languages, home economics, mathematics, physical education, reading, science, social studies, and the evaluation of training. Each reference listed contains sample items, instruments, or frameworks for assessment that can be freely adapted. A few of the publications list sources of *unpublished* instruments. Many contain advice on what to do and what not to do when measuring the subject field. The validity of the instruments put at your disposal through these books may or may not be well established.

Section 2 lists articles and books that explain how to construct written tests, regardless of subject and how to convert raw scores to norm scores, should the need arise.

A list of publishers who offer to "do it all" for you constitutes Section 3. These test services will put together a test to your specifications, to fit your program.

Finally, the last section lists articles and books for further reading. These should enable you to find out more about major concepts and issues in achievement testing, and particularly about the relevance of criterion-referenced and norm-referenced approaches to test construction and score interpretation.

As a check on the quality of the items in the test or of the assessment tasks you do eventually produce, consult Appendix B, page 159, "A Reminder of Some Common Item Construction Errors."

Section 1. Subject-Oriented Publications on How to Assess Performance

The Arts

Stake, R. E. et al. (1975). *Evaluating the arts in education: A responsive approach.* Columbus, OH: Charles E. Merrill.

Chapters by several authors in this book explore the problem of just what an evaluator should consider in assessing the arts in schools. "Arts" is intended to encompass graphic arts, theatre, dance, music, film, and television. The chapters by Stake and McLean should be particularly helpful in terms of suggesting an overall approach to evaluating arts education.

The responsive evaluation advocated by Stake devotes much time to observing the program in action, identifying issues that confront the program participants, addressing the questions that various evaluation audiences want answered, and interpreting the program as witnessed in light of the different value-perspectives inferred by the evaluator.

The chapter by L. D. McLean on "judging the quality of a school as a place where the arts might thrive" calls the evaluator's attention to the school environment as a whole, the suitability and accessibility of the work space allotted to arts activities, the artistic output of the school, and the support shown for artistic activities and output. McLean provides a series of charts that summarize the facts and judgments that such an evaluation should take into account.

The book ends with a bibliography that includes abstracts of 28 readings in evaluation and arts education, annotated references for 10 evaluation reports, 62 references for topics of interest, and descriptive references for 9 other sourcebooks that could be helpful to an evaluator of arts education.

Thomas, R. M. (1965). Rationale for measurement in the visual arts. *Educational and Psychological Measurement, 25*(1), 163-189.

After reviewing the chief faults of most art tests, the author proposes four features that should characterize future attempts at measurement in art:

(1) provision for measuring a greater variety of factors that compose products and art abilities;
(2) more adequate distinctions among the abilities involved in appreciation, criticism, and production of art;
(3) test norms that are adaptable to different schools or philosophies of art;
(4) a more adequate treatment of the creativity dimension.

The author then attempts to outline strategies for constructing tests that accomplish the first three of these goals, while admitting that his proposal "does relatively little to solve the problem of measuring creativity."

The author discusses separately measures of art preference, art analysis, and art production, which he says are needed to measure both aptitude and achievement. In each of these three categories, he provides illustrative items, describes the range of content coverage that he thinks is desirable, and discusses considerations of test format and administration.

Evaluators of programs in the visual arts will appreciate this article either for its advice concerning test construction or for its provision of models and standards against which to assess published instruments.

Career and Vocational Education

Hardaway, M. (1966). *Testing and evaluation in business education.* Cincinnati, OH: Southwestern Publishing.

After discussing general considerations involved in the development of a testing program and the construction of tests, the author provides many types of sample test items for measuring business, bookkeeping and accounting, clerical and secretarial knowledge and skills, as well as a few items dealing with personnel communication, office management, and other topics relevant to business education.

Warmbrod, J. R. (1974). *Criterion-referenced instruments for assessment of specialized vocational agricultural programs: Final report.* Columbus: Ohio State University, Dept. of Agricultural Education. (Abstract in *Resources in Education*, 1976, *11*(3). ED 113 547.)

According to the ERIC abstract, "criterion referenced, field-tested instruments developed to assess 11th and 12th grade vocational agricultural education programs in (1) agricultural mechanics, (2) horticulture, (3) agribusiness supplies and services, and (4) farm management are presented in the document. A narrative report briefly discusses objectives; test construction; field testing, which involved administering the test to 12th grade students in 16 area vocational centers and 10 local schools; and the program's contribution to education. Appended materials make up the body of the document . . . and consist of: an extensive treatment of test objectives and the mastery tests for each of the four areas, a list of schools in which field testing was done, and 24 tables giving item analysis and summary statistics for each test."

Vocational Competency Measures Project. (1976). American Association for Vocational Instructional Materials, 120 Driftmier Engineering Center, Athens, GA 30602.

This association has 17 vocational competency measures available, including tests for computer operator, word processing specialist, grocery clerk, dental assistant, restaurant services, carpenter and diesel mechanic. Test booklets and specimen sets are available upon request.

English and Language Arts

Bock, D., & Bock, H. (1981). *Evaluating classroom speaking.* Annandale, VA: Speech Communication Association.

The authors survey recent research and practice in assessing oral communication performances in the classroom, including a discussion of rater errors. They also provide 13 different evaluation forms and a chapter on constructing your own form.

Cooper, C. R. (1977). Holistic evaluation of writing. In C. R. Cooper & L. Odell, *Evaluating writing: Describing, measuring, judging.* Urbana, IL: National Council of Teachers of English.

This chapter provides a number of rating scales and dichotomous (yes/no) scales for making a series of overall judgments about a piece of student writing. The scales included were designed for three types of writing: expository (explanatory) writing, personal narrative writing, and dramatic writing. The author argues for the validity of these procedures, and discusses methods for improving the reliability of rater judgments.

Cooper, C. R. (Ed.). (1981). *The nature and measurement of competency in English.* Urbana, IL: National Council of Teachers of English.

This book presents an in-depth look at the issues associated with developing language arts competency tests. Two chapters of particular interest are "Competence in Reading" (Alan Purves, pp. 65-94) and "Defining and Assessing Competence in Writing" (Lee Odell, pp. 95-138).

Diederich, P. B. (1974). *Measuring growth in English.* Urbana, IL: National Council of Teachers of English.

The author's major purpose is to provide procedures for making essay grading more reliable. The book includes descriptive criteria that can be used by raters to determine the level of adequacy of a piece of writing with respect to eight factors. The author also discusses how to establish acceptable topics for test essays and maintain secrecy in the final determination of the stimulus content of the essay test. The book ends with 96 statements of qualities that are usually desirable in writing, some of which may be useful as objectives in teaching writing skills.

Fagan, W. T., Cooper, C. R., & Jensen, J. M. (1975). *Measures for research and evaluation in the English language arts.* Urbana, IL: ERIC Clearinghouse on Reading and Communication Skills and National Council of Teachers of English.

This book systematically describes 87 instruments that test various aspects of English language arts education. Among these instruments are 23 tests of reading skills, 15 tests of achievement in literature, 14 tests of language development, 14 tests of writing skills, and 9 tests of standard English as a second language or dialect. Information is provided about each instrument's purpose; when it was constructed; the appearance, organization, and administration of the items; the nature and extent of validity, reliability, and normative data available; and how to order the instrument. Also, in the majority of cases, the book includes sample items from the tests.

In order to be selected for inclusion in the book, each of the 87 instruments was first judged

- "suitable for assessing a component of the field of English education,"
- "readily available to the potential user," and
- "*not* available commercially."

The authors' intention was to make accessible to language arts teachers a variety of potential achievement measures.

Myers, M. (1980). *A procedure for writing assessment and holistic scoring.* Urbana, IL: National Council of Teachers of English.

This manual deals with the development of direct assessments of writing ability. It provides guidance in topic selection, the development of test directions, the establishment of test conditions, holistic scoring procedures, and score reporting.

Rubin, D., & Mead, N. (1984). *Large-scale assessment of oral communication skills: Kindergarten through grade 12.* Annandale: VA: Speech Communication Association.

The authors review 45 testing instruments for measuring students' speaking and listening skills.

Quellmalz, E., & Burry, J. (1983). Analytic scales for assessing students' expository and narrative writing skills.

This paper describes analytic scales and reliable scoring procedures for assessing students' expository and narrative composition. The scales are criterion referenced and provide diagnostic feedback for individual students and for program analysis.

Spandel, V., & Stiggins, R. J. (1980). *Direct measures of writing skill: Issues and applications.* Portland, OR: Northwest Regional Educational Laboratory.

This booklet provides a comprehensive overview of the issues associated with developing direct assessments of writing performance. The issues discussed include direct versus indirect writing assessment, reliability and validity, developing exercises, scoring procedures (holistic, analytic, primary trait, scoring language usage and mechanics), a comparison of scoring methods, and using writing tests to evaluate programs.

Special Issue on Writing Assessment (1984). *Educational Measurement: Issues and Practice, 3.*

This special issue of *Educational Measurement* contains articles on various aspects of developing and administering large-scale writing assessments. These articles include "Issues in Direct Writing Assessment: Problem Identification and Control" by Vana H. Meredith and Paul L. Williams; "Scoring Direct Writing Assessments: What Are the Alternatives?" by Ina V. S. Mullis; "The Application of Direct Writing Assessments in Five States" by Paul L. Williams; and "Toward Successful Large-Scale Writing Assessment: Where Are We Now? Where Do We Go from Here?" by Edys S. Quellmalz.

Foreign Languages

Valette, R. M. (1977). *Modern language testing.* New York: Harcourt Brace Jovanovich.

Although this book contains some general advice concerning measurement of achievement in foreign language education, it is primarily a resource of *item types* suitable for testing various aspects of foreign language learning. The important features of each item type are described, and a sample is then provided in most cases.

Item types are provided for listening comprehension, speaking, reading comprehension, writing competence, comprehension of the culture, and knowledge of literature. In addition, several scales are provided for rating proficiency in speaking a foreign language. The final chapter provides seven item types for constructing an informal oral test of bilingual competence in listening and speaking.

In an appendix on commercially available language tests, the author describes various tests of foreign languages under the headings "achievement tests" and "proficiency tests." The languages covered by these tests are French, Spanish, German, Russian, Italian, and Hebrew. A majority of these instruments test listening, reading, and writing skills; a minority also test speaking skills. Other tests described are general prognostic language aptitude tests, tests of English as a second language, a Spanish/English bilingual test for K-2, and a foreign language attitude questionnaire. All these commercially available tests are described rather than evaluated, and neither validity nor reliability information is provided.

Home Economics

Indiana Home Economics Association. (1974). *Evaluation in home economics.* West Lafayette, IN: University Book Store. (Abstract in *Resources in Education*, 1975, *10*(12). ED 109 334.)

The instruments included in this book are intended as resources for the evaluation of students and programs with respect to home economics education. The book begins with a discussion of tests, checklists, rating scales, and questionnaires. The authors recommend the use of a variety of measures in order adequately to assess different aspects of the program. The remainder of the book consists of sample instruments with suggestions for their use in evaluating knowledge and attitudes in the areas of child development, clothing and textiles, consumer education, foods and nutrition, housing and home decoration, and interpersonal relations.

While several of the sample instruments might be used in an evaluation study of a home economics program, most of the instruments appear to be more suitable as instructional aids than as evaluation tools. The tests do, however, sample a range of skills and possible instructional objectives; and they could serve as a basis for discussing which objectives are most crucial and which understandings and skills are most lacking in the students. After such an assessment of student needs, a critical review of the items in these instruments could help an evaluator in constructing a valid measure of the skills addressed by the program.

Mathematics

Suydam, M. N. (1974). *Unpublished instruments for evaluation in mathematics education: An annotated listing.* Columbus, OH: ERIC

Information Analysis Center for Science, Mathematics and Environmental Education.

This list of tests is "intended as a reference [with] no endorsement . . . implied." References to 208 instruments relevant to math education are annotated. Each annotation contains a statement of what the instrument is designed to measure, the types of items, their format and number, the grade or age level with which the test has been used, and reliability and validity data.

Of the 208 annotated instruments, 172 are cognitive, 26 are affective, 7 are for analysis of teaching, and 3 are for research analysis. Of the cognitive tests, 7 are of algebra, 5 are of creativity, 7 are diagnostic, 7 are of preschool knowledge, 10 are of fractions, 41 are general, 16 are of geometry, 4 are of logic, 4 are of measurement, 4 are designed for mentally retarded students, 3 are of teaching methodology, 18 are of number systems, 7 are of operations (+, −, ×), 12 are Piagetian-related, 6 are of problem-solving, 6 are reading-related, 2 are science-related, and 13 are miscellaneous. All annotated instruments are indexed by type and by author.

Many instruments are cited on a supplementary list; but these are only referenced, not described in detail.

Physical Education

American Alliance for Health, Physical Education and Recreation. (1976). *Testing for impaired, disabled, and handicapped individuals.* Washington, DC: Author.

This booklet gives descriptive and evaluative information about tests in three categories:

- Physical fitness tests (13 tests reviewed). Preceding the descriptions of each test, a comparative overview of their content is provided.
- Motor ability, perceptual motor development, and psychomotor tests (27 tests reviewed). A chart comparing coverage of these tests with respect to 13 component skills (including visual, auditory, tactile, and coordination skills) precedes the separate descriptions of the tests.
- Developmental profiles (9 tests reviewed). Their content is compared and analyzed in terms of the following aspects of development: adaptive behavior, basic knowledge, communication, fine and gross motor skills, personal/social and practical skills, reasoning, self-care, and visual perception.

Each test description lists what is measured and tells how it is measured and how the test is administered and scored.

Finally, 10 locally developed assessment devices are presented at the end of the booklet "to show a variety of locally developed devices and approaches used for both formal testing and informal assessment purposes."

Hunsicker, P., & Reiff, G. G. (1975). *Youth fitness test manual.* Washington, DC: American Alliance for Health, Physical Education, and Recreation.

This booklet presents six tests of physical fitness with accompanying percentile norms based on national samples for ages 10 through 17. Separate norms for males and females are provided. The first test is really two different tests: "pull up: boys" and "flexed-arm hang: girls." The other tests (sit-up, shuttle run, standing broad jump, 50 yard dash, and 600 yard run-walk) are the same for both sexes. Complete directions for administering all tests are provided.

Percentiles for each age are supplemented by percentiles based on a classification index that takes age, height, and weight into account.

Johnson, B. L., & Nelson, J. K. (1974). *Practical measurements for evaluation in physical education.* Minneapolis, MN: Burgess.

This book describes a host of tests in the field of physical education, in many cases providing norms and complete instructions for carrying out the tests. Where this is not done, bibliographic references are supplied. Some of the tests only have norms for college men and women, but others include norms for a broad range of ages.

In addition to describing and referencing a variety of physical fitness and motor ability test batteries, measures of particular physical factors are included in the book. The authors describe 8 tests of flexibility, 10 of strength, 9 of muscular endurance, 6 of cardiovascular condition, 6 of power, 7 of agility, 8 of balance, 7 dealing with reaction and/or speed, 6 of rhythm and dance, 8 rating scales and 9 objective instruments for measuring posture, 4 tests of kinesthetic perception, and 3 perceptual-motor test batteries.

In a long chapter on sports skills, tests for skills in the sports of archery, badminton, basketball, football, golf, gymnastics for women, soccer, softball and baseball, tennis, and volleyball are presented—with norms; and tests for skills in bowling, handball, speedball, and swimming are described with references to sources of more information.

The book provides descriptions, sample items, and references for six measures dealing with leadership, social behavior, and acceptance of status within a group. In addition, one measure of attitude toward physical education is presented in its entirety, and seven other attitude scales dealing with sports and physical activity are described, along with sample items and sources for obtaining entire instruments.

Finally, the authors include a bibliography of journals and theses containing tests of knowledge of particular sports and of topics in physical education.

Reading

Miller, W. H. (1974). *Reading diagnostic kit.* New York: Center for Applied Research in Education.
Potter, T. C., & Rae, G. (1973). *Informal reading diagnosis: A practical guide for the classroom teacher.* Englewood Cliffs, NJ: Prentice-Hall.

These two books are similar in content. They can both serve as a source of informal reading tests that can be freely reproduced or adapted to local needs. There are instruments in both books that measure oral and silent reading skills, word recognition or decoding skills, and attitudes and interests related to reading.

The book by Miller includes a number of reading-observation checklists and projective-technique instruments to help determine causes of reading difficulties. Miller also provides descriptive evaluations of six standardized reading tests and two listening-comprehension tests.

The book by Potter and Rae contains other kinds of instruments related to reading, such as tests measuring auditory, visual, and tactile discrimination; memory; listening and repeating; generative language skills; following directions; listening comprehension; study skills; and literary interpretation.

Science

Berey, D. (1976). *Earth science* (High School Exams and Answer Series, Grades 9-12). Woodbury, NY: Barron's Educational Series.
Edwards, G., & Blifield, M. (1977). *Biology* (High School Exams and Answer Series). Woodbury, NY: Barron's Educational Series.
Gerwitz, H. (1976). *Physics* (Regents Exams and Answer Series, Grades 10-12). Woodbury, NY: Barron's Educational Series.
Test item book for biological science: Inquiry into life. (1968). Boulder, CO: Biological Sciences Curriculum Study.
Test item book for biological science: Molecules to man. (1973).

Boulder, CO: Biological Sciences Curriculum Study.
Test item book for biological science: An ecological approach. (1973).
Boulder, CO: Biological Sciences Curriculum Study.
Walsh, M. J. (1977). *Chemistry* (High School Exams and Answer Series, Grades 9-12). Woodbury, NY: Barron's Educational Series, 1977.

The titles listed above are all sources of test items for measuring basic cognitive learning in science courses at the secondary school level. Program evaluators may want to use these tests as a basis for generating new test items that more closely match the program being studied.

Mayer, V. J. (1974) *Unpublished evaluation instruments in science education: A handbook.* Columbus: ERIC/ SMEAC Reference Center, Ohio State University, College of Education.

Each of the science education instruments described in this guide employs an objective scoring system. None of them is commercially published. Most of the instruments referenced are available from the ERIC Document Service, or a journal, author, or sponsoring institution. Those that are not are included in their entirety in the appendix of the instruments handbook itself.

Every instrument description tells what the instrument measures; the number and types of items and subtests; the educational level (and, in some cases, the geographic area) of the students with whom the test has been used; the reliability data reported and the size of the group used for determining reliability; means and standard deviations of groups tested, where available; procedures used for validating the instrument, if any; and how to acquire a copy of the instrument.

The instruments are organized into six groups. The first group deals with knowledge and understanding of ideas, facts, and principles. The first chapter describes 21 tests of this kind in biology, 22 in earth science, 49 in physics and chemistry, and 26 in general science.

The second group of tests deals with "the ability to effectively engage in the processes and skills involved in scientific inquiry." A total of 32 tests of this type are described.

The third group of instruments deals with student characteristics relevant to science education, such as cognitive preferences, critical thinking, and creative thinking. The volume reviews 16 instruments of this kind.

The fourth group of instruments attempts to measure student attitudes and interests related to science. This group consists of 26 instruments that focus on science or scientists; 22 that focus on taking science classes or being a science teacher; and 10 that focus on conversation, drug abuse, environment, radioactivity, and sex.

The fifth group of tests measures knowledge of the nature and limits of scientific pursuits and of their interrelationship with other social and economic processes. A total of 15 measures of this type are described.

The sixth group of instruments deals with the pedagogy of science education. Listed are 21 instruments that focus on perceptions of science classroom practices, 10 on attitudes toward classroom practices and curricula, 6 on teacher supervision and evaluation, 5 on course content, 1 on teacher expectations of students, and 1 on facilities for science education.

Social Studies

National Council for the Social Studies. (1965). *Thirty-fifth yearbook: Evaluation in social studies.* Washington, DC: Author.

There are many chapters in this yearbook that suggest useful measurement techniques and illustrate principles with sample test items. The following chapters appear to be particularly helpful:

- "The Objective Test Item," H. D. Berg, pp. 47-76.
- "Evaluation of Critical Thinking in the Social Studies," H. M. Chausow, pp. 77-99.
- "Improving the Essay Test in the Social Studies," R. J. Solomon, pp. 137-153.
- "Planning, Assembling, and Administering the Objective Test," pp. 174-201.

As this book was published in 1965, the bibliography of published tests is somewhat dated. However, if used in conjunction with some of the more recent editions of the reference tools cited in Chapter 2, such as Hoepfner or Buros, the descriptive survey provided by this bibliography can still be useful.

Senathirajah, N., & Weiss, J. (1971). *Evaluation in geography: A resource book for teachers.* Toronto: Ontario Institute for Studies in Education.

Three chapters give practical assistance to the evaluator who wants to construct a written test in geography. Examples of a variety of cognitive objectives in geography are included, showing how test items of both the multiple-choice variety and the fill-in type can measure the attainment of complex understandings as well as simple knowledge. The authors also provide suggestions for more reliable scoring of short essay responses to questions in geography. The book includes brief discussions of categorization schemes for objectives and plans for developing a test-item pool from which to sample in putting together a well-balanced test.

Social education. (1976). *Journal of the National Council for the Social Studies, 40*(Nov.-Dec.), 503-541 and 567-582.

This issue has two sections that deal with measuring achievement in social studies. The first section, "Testing in the Social Studies," is intended "to provide ideas and information about social studies test development that teachers might find useful in their classroom situations." The topics included are rationales for testing; standardized tests; and teacher-made tests in world history, American history, political science, economics, and multi-ethnic studies. Illustrative sample items are included in the articles on teacher-made tests.

The second relevant section, "Social Studies and the Elementary Teacher: Informal Assessment of Social Studies Learning," tries to provide "a rationale . . . and examples of techniques and procedures" for evaluation of elementary school students' learning in social studies. The examples were developed and used by teachers. Four evaluation strategies are outlined, and different ways of obtaining and recording meaningful data are illustrated.

This sourcebook should be of assistance in deciding what instruments or strategies to use in measuring achievement in the social studies. For more information, contact the consortium.

Training

Evaluating the impact of training: A collection of federal agency evaluation practices. (1983). Springfield, VA: National Technical Information Service.

This publication reports the efforts of several government agencies to determine the impact of their training programs. The types of courses evaluated include new officer training, supervisory skills training, career development, desk audit training, and management training. Government agencies represented include Department of Agriculture, Department of Education, General Accounting Office, Department of Labor, Department of Navy, National Aeronautics and Space Administration, Department of Treasury, and Office of Personnel Management.

Evaluation procedures described include questionnaires, interviews, performance observations, examples of on-the-job changes, and application of skills on the job.

Section 2. Readings in How to Construct and Norm a Performance Test

How-To Guides to Testing in General

Berk, R. A. (Ed.) (1985). *A guide to criterion-referenced test construction.* Baltimore, MD: Johns Hopkins University Press.

Educational Testing Service. (1973). *Making the classroom test: A guide for teachers.* Princeton, NJ: Author. (Abstract in *Research in Education,* 1974, *9*(1). ED 081 784.)

Gronlund, N. E. (1977). *Constructing achievement tests.* Englewood Cliffs, NJ: Prentice-Hall.

Nitko, A. J. (1983). *Educational tests and measurements: An introduction.* New York: Harcourt Brace Jovanovich.

Payne, D. A. (1974). Constructing short-answer achievement items; constructing and scoring essay items and tests. In *Assessment of learning: Cognitive and affective* (pp. 95-148). Lexington, MA: D.C. Heath.

Roid, G. H., & Haladyna, T. M. (1982). A technology for test-item writing. New York: Academic Press.

Wesman, A. G. (1971). Writing the test item. In R. L. Thorndike (Ed.), *Educational measurement* (pp. 81-129). Washington, DC: American Council on Education.

Writing and Revising Multiple-Choice and True-False Items

Corbluth, J. (1975). Functional analysis of multiple-choice questions for reading comprehension. *English Language Teachers Journal, 29,* 164-173.

Ebel, R. L. (1972). How to write multiple-choice test items. In *Essentials of educational measurement* (pp. 187-225). Englewood Cliffs, NJ: Prentice-Hall.

Ebel, R. L. (1971). How to write true-false items. *Educational and Psychological Measurement, 31,* 417-426.

Roid, G. H., & Haladyna, T. M. (1982). *A technology for test item writing* (chap. 4). New York: Academic Press.

Derivation of Norm Scores With Locally Constructed Instruments

Ebel, R. L. (1972). Percentile ranks; interpretation of percentile ranks; stanine standard scores. In *Essentials of educational measurement* (pp. 285-296). Englewood Cliffs, NJ: Prentice-Hall.

Gronlund, N. E. (1977). Norm-referenced interpretation. In *Constructing achievement tests* (pp. 120-129). Englewood Cliffs, NJ: Prentice-Hall.

Section 3. Producers of Made-To-Order Tests

CTB/McGraw-Hill
Del Monte Research Park
Monterey, California 93940

Houghton-Mifflin Company
777 California Avenue
Palo Alto, California 94304

Intran Corporation
4555 West 77th Street
Minneapolis, MN 55435

IOX Assessment Associates
Box 24095
Los Angeles, California 90024

Measurement Incorporated
2402 Reichard Street, Suite B
Durham, North Carolina 27705

National Evaluation Systems, Inc.
P.O. Box 226
Amherst, Massachusetts 01002

Science Research Associates
155 North Wacker Drive
Chicago, Illinois 60606

For Further Reading

Anderson, R. C. (1972). How to construct achievement tests to assess comprehension. *Review of Educational Research, 42*, 145-170.

Angoff, W. H. (1974). Criterion-referencing, norm-referencing, and the SAT. *College Board Review, 92*, 3-5.

Angoff, W. H. (1971). Scales, norms and equivalent scores. In R. L. Thorndike (Ed.), *Educational measurement* (pp. 508-600). Washington, DC: American Council on Education.

Baker, E. L. (1974). Beyond objectives: Domain-referenced tests for evaluation and instructional improvement. *Educational Technology, 14*(6), 10-16.

Berk, R.A. (Ed.). (1980). *Criterion-referenced measurement: State of the art.* Baltimore, MD: Johns Hopkins University Press.

Bormuth, J. R. (1970). *On the theory of achievement test items.* Chicago: University of Chicago Press.

Brennan, R. L. (1975). Model for the use of achievement data in an instructional system. *Instructional Science, 4*(2), 113-136.

Buros, O. K. (1977). Fifty years in testing: Some reminiscences, criticisms, and suggestions. *Educational Researcher, 6*(7), 9-15.

Ebel, R. L. (1972). Criterion-referenced and norm-referenced measurements. In *Essentials of educational measurement* (2nd ed., pp. 83-86). Englewood Cliffs, NJ: Prentice-Hall.

Ebel, R. L. (1982). Proposed solutions to two problems of test construction. *Journal of Educational Measurement, 19*, 267-278.

Glaser, R., & Nitko, A. J. (1971). Measurement in learning and instruction. In R. L. Thorndike (Ed.), *Educational measurement* (pp. 625-670). Washington, DC: American Council on Education.

Hambleton, R. K. (Ed.). (1983). *Applications of item response theory.* Vancouver, BC: Educational Research Institute of British Columbia.

Hambleton, R. K., & DeGruijter, D.N.M. (1983). Application of item response models to criterion-referenced test item selection. *Journal of Educational Measurement, 20*, 355-367.

Hambleton, R. K., & Eigor, D. R. (1978). Guidelines for evaluating criterion-referenced tests and test manuals. *Journal of Educational Measurement, 15*, 321-327.

Hively, W. (Ed.). (1974). *Domain referenced testing.* Englewood Cliffs, NJ: Educational Technology Publications.

Lord, F. M. (1980). *Applications of item response theory to practical testing problems.* Hillsdale, NJ: Lawrence Erlbaum.

McClelland, D. C. (1973). Testing for competence rather than for "intelligence." *American Psychologist, 28*, 1-14.

Millman, J. (1974). Program assessment, criterion-referenced tests, and things like that. *Educational Horizons, 52*(4), 188-192.

Popham, W. J. (1981). *Modern educational measurement.* Englewood Cliffs, NJ: Prentice-Hall.

Popham, W. J., & Husek, T. R. (1969). Implications of criterion-referenced measurement. *Journal of Educational Measurement, 6*(1), 1-9.

Sanders, J. R., & Murray, S. L. (1976). Alternatives for achievement testing. *Educational Technology, 16*(3), 17-23.

Chapter 5
Validity and Reliability of Performance Instruments

The purpose of this chapter is to present you with an informal introduction to the subjects of reliability and validity. You might use the information here either as a guide for determining the quality of the instruments you construct yourself, or as a set of general principles to bear in mind when reading and interpreting the manuals that accompany the tests you select or in selecting and interpreting other performance indicators. To give you a concrete situation on which to pin the new information presented here, try to read with a particular performance test in mind, imagining how the discussion applies to *it*.

Assessments of validity and reliability help to determine the amount of faith people should place in a measurement instrument. *Validity* and *reliability* refer to different aspects of a measure's or an indicator's *believability*. Judgments of *validity* answer the question, Is the instrument an appropriate one for what needs to be measured? *Reliability* indices answer the question, Does the instrument yield consistent results? For obvious reasons, these are questions you must ask about any measure you select or use, whether you buy it or construct it yourself. It may be helpful to remember that *valid* has the same root as *valor* and *value*, referring to strength or worth. Validity indicates how worthwhile a measure is likely to be, in a given situation, for telling you what you need to know. Validity boils down to whether the instrument is giving you the true story, or at least something approximating the truth.

Reliability, when used to refer to tests, carries the same meaning as when it refers to friends. A reliable friend is one on whom you can count to behave the same way time and again. Tests or indicators that give you essentially the same results when readministered are reliable in this sense.

Please note that reliability refers to consistency, but consistency does not guarantee *truthfulness*. A friend, for instance, who compliments your taste in clothes each time he sees you is certainly reliable but may not necessarily be telling the truth. What is more, he may not even be deliberately misleading you. It may just be a habit, or perhaps his judgment is skewed by an appreciation of your many other good features. It could be that both you and your friend have terrible taste when viewed from some broader perspective! Similarly, an instrument's being reliable does *not* mean that it is a good measure of what it seems to measure.

Is a valid measure reliable? In general, yes. A valid test is one that has demonstrated its power to detect some *real* ability, attitude, or prevailing situation that the test user can identify and characterize. If the ability or skill being measured is itself stable, and if respondents' answers to the items are not affected by other unpredictable factors, then each administration of the instrument should yield essentially the same results.

A demonstration of reliability, therefore, is necessary but not conclusive evidence that an instrument is valid. All the reliability studies in the world will not guarantee validity—though they will help support a strong case for it. Bear this in mind particularly when reading about the technical adequacy of published tests. Since reliability is easier to demonstrate than validity, the technical manuals that accompany tests often report reliability data only. The publisher intends to imply validity through a demonstration of reliability. This is poor practice and amounts to doing half the job. Administrators need more adequate information if they are to justify using the test for making important decisions.

Validity: Is the Instrument an Appropriate One to Measure What You Want to Know?

Time and effort are invested in measurement for one of two reasons:

(1) There is a need to detect *how much* of something—a skill, attitude, or ability—a person has. This is a descriptive function of measurement. Both normed and criterion-referenced performance tests are commonly used to assess how much knowledge or skill a person has acquired, though the *standards* used to decide successful performance differ.

(2) There is a need to predict some *other*, possibly future, performance or state of the person, usually for the purpose of making a decision about that individual. When a test serves a predictive function, the primary interest is in obtaining a sample of present behavior upon which to base

an expectation about how a person will perform in another, more complex setting. This is the case with test use for making decisions about placement in special programs.

When you use a test, you want to know you can rely on it to accomplish one of these two things. In either case, the instrument must provide a *sample of behavior* that supports conclusions about performance in a broader, more real-life context. The validity of a test reflects the sureness with which you can draw such conclusions. In fact, it will serve you well to think of validity as *the extent to which you can rule out interpretations of an instrument's results other than the one you wish to make.* Establishing a test's validity requires that you anticipate the potential arguments skeptics might use to dismiss its results. The credibility of your evaluation will be profoundly affected by the perceived validity of your measures. For this reason, you should include an assessment, even if informal, of each test's validity in your evaluation report. *Five major* approaches to determining if an instrument is valid have evolved. Each represents a different aspect of the problem of building a case for the appropriateness of the test for given situations. Three of the approaches have derived from using tests for description— determining how much of a skill people possess. The fourth approach focuses on the usefulness of the test as a predictor of future behavior. The fifth approach requires a judgment as to the legality of the test for making particular decisions.

Approach 1. Descriptive Use of an Instrument: Construct Validity

The word *construct* is a handy one for discussing measurement instruments. It is a catchall term used to refer to the skill, attitude, or ability that an instrument is intended to measure. "Ability to add decimals," "attitude toward school," "managerial effectiveness," and "spatial ability" are all constructs. *The construct validity of a test is the extent to which you can be sure it represents the construct whose name appears in its title.* In a criterion-referenced test, construct validity means how well the test matches the objectives it is supposed to measure. A test with good construct validity can be considered a substitute for actually observing a person displaying the skill in everyday life. To defend adequately the construct validity of the test, other explanations for what the test measures must be satisfactorily ruled out.

The ease of demonstrating construct validity for a particular instrument depends largely on the specificity of the construct itself.

Sometimes the construct to be measured is one for which representative test items can be written with reasonable ease. This is the case with the ability to multiply fractions, answer questions about bonds in organic chemistry, or take shorthand dictation. In these situations, most people can agree about what a demonstration of the construct's existence would look like. Therefore, defending the instrument's validity simply requires describing how the instrument was developed and administered and comparing it with similar published instruments, if such exist.

Often, though, the construct to be measured is fuzzy, imprecise, or complex. This is particularly the case when a test is needed to measure *higher order* skills such as problem solving, essay writing, creativity, and other representations of complex human performance. No clear, widely accepted definitions yet exist for these. In such cases, demonstrating construct validity demands a preliminary step—precise construct definition.

Construct definition. Before the validity of a test can be determined— actually before the test is developed—the construct that it measures must be defined as precisely as possible.[1] Defining the construct means explaining what is meant by, say, "good narrative style," "creative problem solving," "healthy habits," "refraining from obsessive behaviors," or "the student will write an original sonnet" and pointing out how this definition might differ from those given by others. The definition should encompass the following:

(1) If the construct in question is a complex one, then it should be depicted by means of a diagram, as in Figure 5, page 100, *showing what a person with more—or perhaps less—of the construct might do.* The diagram shows the construct's subcomponents composed of simpler and more discrete behaviors. An evaluator developing a *single* general test or indicator for assessing the whole construct would have to make sure the instrument covered all its subcomponents. Or the developer could write short separate tests to measure one or two subcomponents at a time. In this case a whole *battery* of measures would address the construct.

(2) A description should be prepared of closely related constructs with which the construct in question might be confused. It should include an argument about why this construct is distinct from those and worthy of separate measurement.

When this construct description underpins a general test of a high-level ability or complex performance, it helps the test developer justify that the skill being measured is a real factor influencing behavior. It does this by requiring that the developer anticipate and answer arguments to the contrary. It must be shown, for example, that the behaviors described as "creative problem solving" are not actually better ascribed to "general intelligence" or "divergent thinking." The developer will also need to answer the challenge that "creative problem solving" is too multifaceted to be measured, since it manifests itself differently in different people.

Once construct definition has been satisfactorily accomplished, the developer must still show that the *test or measure itself* is valid. This means that the test measures the degree of presence of the construct that has been defined. Usually, showing construct validity of an instrument amounts to demonstrating that it overcomes extraneous sources of bias, such as ability to "psych out the test" and give only desirable answers, and that its scores are closely related to scores on other measures of the construct.

Be careful that the test you choose for your evaluation is construct valid for your particular purpose. In other words, make sure the construct underlying the test is the one you want to measure. If, for instance, you want to know how adequately a vocational education program has prepared students to read and write on the job, then the test must address itself to *the real-world construct*, not merely to the content of the course of instruction given via the program. This is another way of saying that a test based only on the program, with items presented in the formats used for instruction, *can be considered valid only for measuring within-program performance.* While within-program performance might well be related to overall performance in the skill area in question, you cannot claim that a program-specific test demonstrates this. When designing a performance test for program evaluation you must decide, then, on the precise nature of the construct to be measured: Do you wish to show that the program has developed participant ability to perform in the world beyond the program, or will you and your audience be satisfied with demonstrating that participants have at least achieved what was taught to them directly? If you have an interest in demonstrating both, of course, this can be done. Address part of your measure to each of the two concerns, or construct separate tests.

Defending construct validity. Armed with a detailed description of the construct to be measured, the test developer can support the validity of a test in several ways:

(1) *Opinions of judges.* Suppose you were preparing a test to determine whether participants in a job training program can write letters of application for jobs. The test might consist of a set of newspaper ads describing fictitious jobs for which students must reply. You can get an idea of the validity of this test by showing it to a group of judges— perhaps program planners, teachers, or employers themselves. Ask the judges to make a list of particular skills related to writing application letters that, in their opinion, will be picked up by the instrument. The test can be considered construct valid to the extent that their lists fit your construct definition. What is more, if the judges' individual conclusions about what the instrument seems to be measuring agree with each other as well, then you have even stronger evidence of construct validity.

Using the opinions of judges to assess an instrument's validity, you should be warned, will produce credible results to the extent that the judges merit the trust of your audience. If the judges themselves lack qualifications, or if they stand to benefit from instrument bias, then their judgments will be vulnerable to challenge.

(2) *Correlations.*[2] Another way of establishing construct validity is to administer a second, different test of the same or a *related* construct to the same group of people. Then the results of the two measures can be correlated. You might, for instance, be able to show that your measure of "effective writing" correlates positively with indicators of other language arts skills such as grammatical usage, effective speech, or high reading aptitude. You might also show that your measure of effective writing has a *negative* correlation with detectors of language arts problems such as diagnostic measures of speech disfunction. A whole methodology using "Multi-Trait, Multi-Method Matrices" (Campbell and Fiske, 1959) has evolved for estimating validity by means of a table of correlations with measures similar to and different from the one in question.

Correlational methods for supporting test validity are not often used with criterion-referenced tests because the scores from these tests may not have sufficient variability to provide a useful correlation coefficient.[3]

(3) *Criterion group studies.* If possible, the test could be administered to a group of people already judged to possess an abundance or deficiency of the construct in question. Demonstrating, for instance, that people reputed to be good writers score well on a "creative writing" test and that people judged low score low builds a strong case for the instrument's validity; similarly, you might show that a particular indicator differentiates between programs that are independently judged as effective, those that are known to have significant problems, or differentials between substance abusers and nonabusers. Criterion group studies are wise to perform, particularly if you are developing an instrument yourself. In addition to assessing validity, they may help you to identify

items that are inadequate for measuring the construct or that give unreliable responses. Discarding these items will improve the quality of the instrument, increasing both its validity and reliability.

(4) *Appeal to logic.* Many times, particularly when the construct can be easily defined, audiences will accept the instrument as logically related to the construct, as long as they know that it has been *administered fairly*, that is:

- Enough time has been allowed for its administration so that the respondents are not rushed.
- Hints and clues about the proper way to answer are absent from the instrument's format or instructions.
- There is no bias in the scoring.

In every instance where you use a test, you are asking not only that the audience accept the instrument's representation of the construct, but also that they accept the *circumstances of its administration*, and do not view these circumstances as having invalidated the results.

Demonstrating a test's construct validity, it should be apparent, is not an all-or-nothing matter. The demonstration can rely on any combination of the types of evidence described here. If you plan to use an instrument more than once, consider the *entire period of its use* an opportunity to collect validity information. Each administration is a chance to find out more about the opinions of judges, the instrument's correlation with the respondents' performance on other measures, and the performance of criterion groups, as well as its concurrent and predictive validity, to be discussed below. Establishing construct validity should be a continuing process.

Approach 2. Descriptive Use of an Instrument: Content Validity

Before an instrument can be written to test for the presence of a particular skill, the construct has to be translated into a set of distinctive *behaviors*. These behaviors are described in terms of how people act, or occasionally, what others tend to say about them. The test itself is then constructed in order to prompt people to display these characteristic behaviors.

Now any complex construct, such as "effective writing ability," will be definable as a collection of several *different* types of behavior; and its accurate detection may even require using more than one kind of measurement instrument. Figure 5, for example, shows a collage of the behaviors that you might decide would collectively indicate that someone writes well.[4] Examining the figure should bring to mind any number of tasks that could be included in tests of effective writing. A complete list of all the relevant tasks would constitute an immense collection. Since no test can encompass all of them, the actual instrument you construct must contain a *sample* of the possible tasks. *Content validity refers to the representativeness* of the sample of questions included in the instrument. If a test is criterion-referenced and addressed to one or two subcomponents, then the test's content validity refers to how representatively its items represent the subconstructs it is intended to assess.

Content validity when a single test is supposed to represent a broad construct

To assure content validity a single general test of effective writing based on Figure 5 would have to do two things:
It should

(1) include tasks that represent the use of skills from all seven categories of behavior to be presented;

(2) give *emphasis* to each category according to its importance in providing evidence of the construct, as depicted in the figure. In cases where the construct to be measured can be divided into discrete and mutually exclusive categories—say, for example, in measuring math skills—this can be controlled by means of the number of questions asked per category or the number of points earned by answering correctly the questions from different categories.

When measuring *complex* skills such as writing—where skills are not discrete and good performance means using different abilities all at once—the task of assuring adequate representation is difficult. There are two possible approaches to this task:

(1) If the test of effective writing you plan to develop will depend on students' producing *writing samples*, then you can assure attention to the seven categories defining the construct by developing scoring criteria that require readers to produce seven separate scores, one for each. These scores could then be *weighted* to produce a final composite test score based on the *proportional* contribution of each category to the overall construct. Looking at Figure 5, this means that "outlines and plans text adequately," a particularly important skill, would be weighted more heavily than "shows adequate vocabulary development," which takes up a smaller proportion of the graph.

(2) You can circumvent the complicated problem of asking for seven separate scores, and then weighting them, by moving some of the more

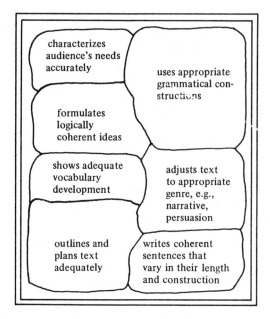

Figure 5. Hypothetical collage of categories of behaviors comprising the construct Effective Writing.
Categories providing stronger evidence of the construct have been assigned a proportionately larger
area.

discrete skills to separate subtests. For instance, your instrument could
include multiple-choice tests of vocabulary and grammar. This would
limit to five the number of score categories for readers and perhaps make
the task of scoring the test slightly easier. In determining the composite
score, however, vocabulary and grammar subtest scores would be
included with the others—again proportionate to their representation in
the overall construct.

   In most performance testing situations, you will have less trouble
accommodating the need for content validity. Consider, for example,
the job of examining the content validity of a test to assess the
effectiveness of a first-year algebra program. The construct, *first-year
algebra*, might break down in a way similar to that shown in the

construct collage in Figure 6. Here units of instruction show relatively discrete and mutually exclusive category areas. Logarithms can be tested separately from quadratic equations; graphing, from positive and negative whole numbers. In this case, proper test emphasis can be controlled by means of the number of questions asked or the number of points assigned to each question in scoring. The test in Figure 6 is content valid. Its high content validity means that the test "maps onto" the collection of possible questions that could be asked about this construct by sampling representatively from its various manifestations.

A measure that focuses too heavily on one category, as in Figure 7, is not content valid for measuring the whole. It is content valid only for the categories it *does* measure. The test in Figure 7, for instance, would be more accurately titled "A Test For Quadratic Equations with a Few Logarithms and Exponents Thrown In."

Content validity when criterion-referenced tests represent subconstructs

A test developer bringing a criterion-referenced test battery for the first-year algebra course depicted in Figure 6 would approach the problem of content validity[5] a little differently from a colleague constructing a single general test. First of all, the battery builder can construct a *separate test* for each discrete behavior category or domain. The concern related to content validity will be *that each test reflects its own category and only its category.* Whereas the general test developer must be concerned that the test's items proportionately represent different, *heterogeneous* behaviors composing the construct, the development of a single highly specific test needs to ensure sameness, or *homogeneity*, of items. *Representativeness of a criterion-referenced test means that all its items reflect the same particular skill or skills.*

As you might have imagined, the need for item homogeneity makes construction of CRTs difficult for complex constructs such as effective writing. An initial temptation might be to define the construct as a thousand small abilities and test all of them! But such a test would almost surely lose its construct validity for describing skills needed in the world beyond the test. The best current solution to the problem of CRTs for complex skills is to do the following:

(1) Break down the complex area into as many discrete domains of performance as you can—say, writing letters, short narratives, arguments, and the like—and try to create separate uniform tests for each.

(2) Score these tests according to separate skill categories as described on pages 99 and 100.

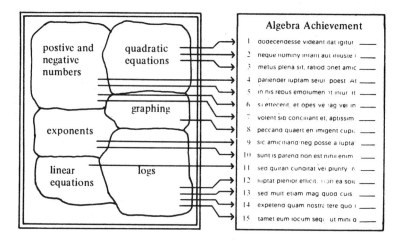

Figure 6. Construct collage for first-year algebra course with front page of a test seeking to have *good content validity*–that is, to proportionately represent each component category of the construct as depicted by the collage. Note that larger categories receive greater emphasis on the test.

A word needs to be said about the accuracy of the construct collages used as a basis for guiding construction of content valid tests. Since little is currently known about the psychological processes contributing to complex skills such as creative problem solving or effective writing, professionals must remain uncertain about which behaviors best reflect their existence. A picture of "effective writing" such as the one in Figure 5, while it might rest on best guesses about the degree of contribution of different abilities to the overall construct, must remain supposition. There is no neat photo of the psyche to serve as the basis for test construction. Thus test builders must either rely on hunches or use fairly technical analytic procedures to define the constructs they aim to assess.[6]

When you attempt to assess the content validity of your own or purchased instruments, the best thing to do is to create for yourself your own mental construct collage and assure yourself that the test or the test battery (1) has not left out any important behaviors and (2) contains the proper proportion of items representing each sub-area of potential behaviors.

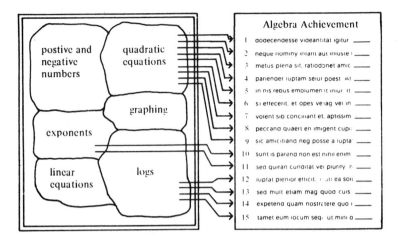

Figure 7. Construct collage for first-year algebra course with achievement test showing poor content validity. The category "quadratic equations" is over-represented, some categories are under-represented, and some are excluded altogether.

Some attempt should be made to demonstrate construct and content validity whenever you discuss the use of an instrument that is intended to describe *how much* of a skill people possess. You will notice that neither form of validity is easy to determine. The best way to describe a test's validity in your report will be to make a list of the *possible challenges* that might be made to its appropriateness for the particular situation, and to marshal the information you have assembled to answer each of them in turn.

Approach 3. Descriptive Use of an Instrument: Concurrent Validity

The concurrent validity of an instrument is established by collecting data to see if the results obtained with the instrument agree with results from other instruments, administered at approximately the same time, to measure the same thing. Let us say, for example, that you have administered a reading pretest to students in a new remedial program. At the same time, the program teachers gave each student an oral reading test that yielded a composite score based on reading fluency, speed, and comprehension. If the reading test and the teachers' oral measures yielded essentially the same results—the same students scored high or low on both measures—then the measures, in effect, have supported each other's validity. Calculating concurrent validity is useful in two situations:

(1) Some circumstances call for a relatively *quick* estimate of the state of people's performance. Concurrent validity is often calculated on a measure that someone has developed in order to shorten the time spent testing. In the reading test example above, the written reading test will save a considerable amount of teacher time and produce similar results.

(2) A demonstration that a test has concurrent validity is good evidence of its construct validity. If it gives you results similar to those from another test, and that test's validity for measuring a particular construct has been fairly well established, then you can build a case that your test also measures the construct. This use of correlational evidence to establish validity is discussed on page 97.

Concurrent validity is determined by calculating a correlation coefficient between results from the instrument in question and results for the same individuals on a different measure of similar or related behavior, where both sets of results are taken to represent the status of individuals during the same period of time. This correlation statistic is then recorded and discussed in the evaluation report. For some pointers about setting up data for calculating a correlation coefficient, see page 114.

Concurrent validity is often calculated for norm-referenced tests; but since criterion-referenced tests usually fail to provide the amount of score variability necessary for correlations, concurrent validity of criterion-referenced tests is seldom discussed.

Approach 4. Decision Related Use of an Instrument: Predictive Validity

Construct, content, and concurrent validity are concerned with how well an instrument represents a person's possession of a certain construct—a skill, attitude, or ability. It often happens that test developers care little about exactly *what* a test measures, preferring to define its value in terms of its ability to *predict future behavior*. For these situations, developers have employed methods for determining predictive validity.

If, for example, students who receive high scores on a high school exit exam later show high achievement in college, one could say that the exit exam distinguishes among those who will or will not do well in pursuing higher education. The test might be used subsequently with comparable accuracy to make similar predictions. Predictive, like concurrent, validity can be calculated and expressed as a *correlation coefficient* relating the instrument in question to a valid measure of the later-occurring predicted behavior.

Predictive validity of a criterion-referenced test could be shown by statistically comparing later performances of people who had either passed or failed it. A test battery's predictive validity might be computed by correlating overall raw score of number of objectives passed with measures of later performance.

Approach 5: Legality of an Instrument: Curricular, Instructional and Job-Related Validity

In recent years tests have increasingly been used for selection, promotion, and certification purposes. For example, many states and local school districts have put in place proficiency assessments that students must pass before they can receive a high school diploma. States have also legislated that teachers must demonstrate their competence in order to be hired or retained. And employers continue to use tests to screen job applicants before employment.

All such uses of tests have been put to repeated legal challenges. These challenges focus on the fairness of a test's contents in relation to the decisions that will be made based upon examinees' performance on the measure. A new interpretation of content validity has emerged out of these challenges: In order for the use of a test to be legal, that test must be an equitable measure of what is taught or what is required on the job. Federal legislation in the form of the *Uniform Guidelines on Employee Selection Procedures* (Equal Employment Opportunity Commission, Civil Service Commission, U.S. Department of Justice and U.S. Department of Labor, 1978) establishes the standard that the skills tested for employment must be the same as the skills demanded by the job. Individual law suits (for example, *Debra P. v. Turlington,* 564 F. Supp. 177 [M.D. Fla. 1983]) have set the precedent that the skills tested for promotion or graduation from public school must have been included in the curriculum as well as actually covered in classroom instruction. Hence the concepts of job-related, curricular, and instructional validity.

These types of content validity typically are determined by various review processes wherein different categories of individuals are asked to judge the contents of a test. In the case of a high school graduation test, curriculum experts might be asked whether the test's contents are part of the stated curriculum, teachers might be asked whether they have offered instruction on the skills tested, and students might be asked whether their schoolwork offered adequate preparation for the examination. In the case of a test used for employment, experienced workers and supervisors might be asked the frequency with which various tested skills are required on the job and the criticality of each to successful work performance. All of these various judgments are then presented in defense of the examination's validity as a certification procedure.

There is no hard and fast rule that states how well a test must match courses of study, instruction, or job requirements for it to be considered valid and legal to use. In conducting these types of validity studies, therefore, the best advice is to gather as many judgments as possible from as wide a range of credible and knowledgeable reviewers as you can identify.

In the best of all possible worlds, each applicable kind of validity would be assessed each time an instrument was used. Rarely is the validity question so thoroughly attacked, however. You will have to be the judge of how much time and effort you can devote to establishing the validity of the instruments you use. Your evaluation report should frankly note validity problems that have to be left unresolved.

Threats to Validity

The following are reasons why efforts to produce valid performance tests might fail:

(1) *Lack of standardization in test administration.* You will remember that test validity depends upon not only the contents of the test but also on *the conditions under which it is administered.* You need to ensure that your test is given in the same way to each group of program participants. To the extent that you allow the method of administration to remain *unprescribed,* you increase the likelihood that test administrators will feel free to introduce instructions or changes, give help or hints, or allow too much time to some respondents. All of these will differentially bias the results.

(2) *Response bias or evaluation apprehension.* Response bias refers to a situation in which people taking a test develop a strategy for responding based on something other than their knowledge of the subject matter or their skill in the construct presumably assessed. The test constructor, for example, may have made the error in a multiple choice test of making "A" the correct answer too often; or perhaps participants have noticed

that the correct answer is the option with the largest number of words. Tests with built-in response bias measure skill in taking tests—not the construct in question. Evaluation apprehension refers to the anxiety many people experience when taking a test for a life-guiding decision. In program evaluation, if the test results will be used for judging only the program and not the individual participant, you should reassure respondents. It is not usually a good idea, on the other hand, to allow test-takers to remain anonymous. This removes a certain amount of motivation to do well and take the test seriously.

(3) *Too few items per objective.* Sometimes performance tests aimed at assessing a broad range of achievement rely on one or two questions or tasks to detect the presence of a particular skill. A single item or task is open to myriad errors not only in interpretation but also in computing or formulating a response. The skeptic can always challenge results from single items on the grounds of indeterminate effects from both random and purposeful errors. Although the *test as a whole* may be a valid measure of performance in the *general* subject area it represents, you will be unable to make a valid judgment about the presence of the particular subskill measured by only one item.

(4) *Tests that measure the skill too narrowly.* Sometimes the inference made from a test score applies to a broader range of abilities than is justified by the comparatively *restricted* nature of the actual test items. A test of ability to *write* that focuses only on paragraphs, for example, is not a valid indicator of ability to write themes. A test that demands *addition of fractions* with a common denominator does not indicate ability to add fractions when the denominators are different.

(5) *Mismatch between the skills called for by the test and the stated objective of the test.* A test, for instance, that requires students to mark an X over words spelled incorrectly does not measure attainment of the objective that students be able to spell the words themselves. Such a test should not, in fact, be called a spelling test if your audience is likely to interpret the results as indicating students' ability to spell words correctly from memory.

(6) *Tests that attempt to measure very complex constructs.* Although some measurement specialists will assert that it is possible to write a test for anything, measures purporting to assess very complex or abstract concepts should be carefully examined before they are accepted for use. Focus your examination on determining whether the test items present a defensible operationalization of the construct under study. For example, if a test is called a measure of "creativity" or "problem solving" or "decision making," do the test items adequately reflect the potential scope of the domain? Or, are they narrow, limited, or otherwise flawed? Does the test developer provide convincing evidence as to why the test is

an appropriate measure of the construct? Negative answers to questions such as these indicate a measure from which you will be unable to draw valid inferences about the construct being considered.

(7) *Tests whose format and wording are tied to the idiosyncrasies of a particular set of instructional materials or of a particular program.* Such tests, often "embedded" within a set of instructional materials, tap to some extent students' mastery of the formats used by the particular materials. For example, students may be instructed to add with materials using a horizontal format—x + y =—rather than a vertical format

$$\begin{array}{r} x \\ + y \\ \hline = \end{array}$$

Since there is no way of knowing *how much* the knowledge of format affects performance, results of these tests are hard to interpret. In an evaluation using a control group, the use of tests embedded in one program is unfair to the participants in the other program.

(8) *Coding and scoring errors.* Mistakes can be made in scoring a test, and such mistakes will reduce the measure's validity. For example, the answer key used to process a set of examinations may give the wrong answer for an item, resulting in inaccurate test scores. Such a scoring key error can exist in commercially published as well as evaluator-prepared performance measures. An important caution to take whenever administering a test is to go through each item and its coded answer to make sure the key is correct. If you have prepared the test yourself, ask several people independently to select the correct answer for each item. Compare the responses from these individuals to verify the accuracy of your answer key.

Summary

Remember that validity has to do with an instrument's appropriateness for accomplishing your purposes. These purposes might be to describe people or to make a decision about them, or both. If you wish to describe them, you want to discuss how much of a skill or ability they have. If you expect your audience to accept the results from an instrument used for this purpose, you need to demonstrate construct, content, or concurrent validity. Construct validity refers to how well the instrument measures what it claims to measure. Demonstrating construct validity demands clear definition of the construct, then presentation of logical arguments, credible opinions, and evidence from correlational or criterion group studies—all aimed at ruling out alternative explanations of the instrument's results. Content validity refers to how well the items give appropriate emphasis to the various components of the construct. To show content validity, you should provide evidence that the instrument contains a set of items that sample the construct's various sub-areas and give each its proportionate emphasis. If the test is criterion-referenced, content validity requires that its items be homogeneous. Concurrent validity is calculated when you use the result of one measure to predict the results of an alternative contemporaneous measure. Predictive validity justifies a test's usefulness for making decisions about people—such as selection for special programs. A case is usually made for predictive validity by demonstrating that the instrument correlates well with valid measures of the behavior it is intended to predict. Curricular, instructional and job-related validity examine the legality of a test's contents in relation to decisions that will be made based upon the test.

The credibility of your evaluation depends on the use of valid instruments. Since there is no established correct method for determining validity, when you select, construct, administer, and interpret your instruments, try to anticipate skepticism about your results; select appropriate methods for investigating possible criticisms; and finally, describe the precautions you have taken and the results of your validity investigation in your evaluation report.

Reliability: Does the Test Produce Consistent Results?

If you were to give students a math test one day and, without additional instruction, give them the same test two days later, you expect each student to receive more or less the same score. If this should turn out *not* to be the case, you would have to conclude that your instrument is *unreliable*, because, without instruction, a person's knowledge of math does not fluctuate much from day to day. If the score fluctuates, then, the problem must be with the test. Its results must be influenced by things other than math knowledge. All these other things are called *error. Reliability refers to the extent to which measurement results are free of unpredictable kinds of error.*

Sources of error that affect reliability include the following:

- fluctuations in mood or alertness of respondents because of illness, fatigue, recent good or bad experiences, or other temporary differences among members of the group being measured;
- variations in the conditions of administration from one testing to the next. These range from various distractions, such as unusual outside

noise, to inconsistencies in the administration of the instrument, such as oversights in giving directions;

- cheating between examinees or help given to respondents by the test administrator (for example, answers provided by the teacher in an attempt to have students achieve higher scores on a test);
- differences in scoring or interpreting results, chance differences in what an observer notices, and errors in computing scores;
- random effects by respondents who guess or check off alternatives without trying to understand them.

Methods for demonstrating an instrument's reliability—whether the instrument is a long and general one or is composed of just a few items—involve comparison of one administration with another administration *to the same people*. This is followed by calculation of a statistic that measures relationships (usually a correlation coefficient) to demonstrate the similarity of two sets of results. The higher the correlation, the smaller the influence of error. Unlike validity, reliability is expressed as a number, usually a *reliability coefficient*, which is a positive decimal less than 1. Like validity, reliability has a long history, and several methods for demonstrating it have evolved. Which one is used will depend partly on the characteristics of the instrument and partly, as usual, on availability of resources such as money and time.

Test-retest reliability is the oldest and most intuitively obvious method for demonstrating instrument consistency. It involves the basic readministration method described above. Readministration must occur, however, within a time period during which the ability, attitude, or skill cannot itself be expected to change. For measuring most constructs, a good rule-of-thumb has been to wait a month between administrations. Readministration to the same group within a few days or weeks presents a problem: How much of what they remember from the first administration has carried over to the second? Even waiting a month does not eliminate this potential challenge, though it reduces its potency. A long time between administrations, on the other hand, raises the possibility that the "true" skill or attitude of the respondents will have changed. In order to divorce reliability measures from either memory effects or real changes, other methods of detecting reliability have been developed.

Alternate-form reliability attacks the problem of memory effects upon the second administration by having the developer create two essentially equivalent forms of the same instrument.[7] Each individual who receives form A on the first occasion will later receive form B, and vice versa. The method does not completely eliminate the effects of memory, since format across forms remains the same, however; and it does demand that time be spent devising extra items and preparing two test forms. In cases where two forms of an instrument have been planned anyway, this kind of check on the reliability of locally produced instruments should be considered.

Split-half reliability yields a measure of test consistency within a single administration.[8] It allows the developer to obtain the two necessary scores from the same group of people by taking two halves of the items composing and instrument and treating them as two administrations. Thus it separates reliability considerations from the effects of learning or developmental change on the respondents. It compares two forms of the test (the two halves) worked on as simultaneously as is humanly possible! Calculating split-half reliability demands, of course, that the questions that compose the two halves be as alike as possible. Otherwise, your calculation of the effect of error will be complicated by a change in real content.[9] Because of this, the split-half method for estimating reliability is best used with instruments that have many items, and where pairs of items can be considered equivalent enough for random distribution to essentially separate forms. These conditions are more likely to be met by items on a test with homogeneous items—such as a general vocabulary test—than by items on a test of a complex skill such as poetry writing or even reading. Then, too, split-half reliability yields a rather specialized sort of information. It tells you whether subgroups of the items on the test yield essentially the same results. A high split-half correlation means that the test is *internally consistent*, to use the nicely descriptive measurement jargon. Internal consistency, which can be measured in several ways other than split-half correlation, refers to the tendency of different items to elicit the same ability or attitude from any given respondent on a single administration of the instrument. It is important to remember, however, that measures of internal consistency do *not* tell you about error that might result from taking the test on different occasions. For this reason, they are *not* a good way to demonstrate reliability if you need to present a case that the instrument is consistent across administrations. Calculations of split-half reliability, in addition, should be supplemented by a statistical adjustment to correct for the small size of the two item pools being compared. Most statistics texts describe this procedure.

Interrater Reliability

Special problems for establishing reliability arise when the "instrument" is actually a *person*, for example, an observer, interviewer, or reader of essay questions. The fact that the perceptions of this person can fluctuate leads to doubts about the accuracy of these measures. Not only may the test environment and the behavior of the person who is being tested vary from time to time; the *perceptions* of the people doing the reporting might diverge as well. That is, two people looking at the same sample of behavior may rate it differently, and the *same* person looking at the *same* sample at different times may arrive at different ratings. The reader of an essay question, for example, might see an answer as indicating "excellent" comprehension of the topic at time A and only "average" at time B.

The best way to demonstrate that your evaluation has been minimally contaminated by inconsistency among "human instruments" is to *have more than one person* perform at least a sample of the observations or the readings that the test requires. If different people report behavior or activities in essentially the same way, then you have evidence that the criteria for scoring have been well learned and uniformly applied by the observers or raters.

If your test uses essay questions, and only a *single* reader, you can estimate this person's reliability in the following way: Train *another person*, who will act as a reliability check, to score the essays in the same way as the principal reader. Then have this person read and rate a representative sample of the essays. The reliability coefficient that you are able to calculate by correlating scores from these two readers will give you an idea of the consistency with which your one observer can be counted on to score the essays accurately.

Incidentally, if you will be able to have *more than one reader or observer score each essay or event* during data collection, it is good practice to include in your evaluation report the *mean* of the scores given by these separate raters. Because this information comes from several sources, it will be more reliable than separate scores.

Precisely *how* to calculate interrater reliability is a question whose answer is long and rich in contingencies. Because the issue is difficult to resolve, your best strategy will be to follow these steps:

- Focus your defense of the measurement method on its *validity*. If you can present good evidence that the scoring system used is appropriate for obtaining accurate information, the issue of reliability will become moot.

- Have a data analyst examine your situation, and then recommend and perform an appropriate test of interrater reliability.

Table 7 shows a data display for organizing score results from two raters in preparation for calculating a coefficient of interrater reliability. The table directs you to compare two judges' answers to each of an instrument's "items." Down the left-hand column, you should list the items on the instrument. Rater X's responses to the item should be shown as X; Y should be Rater Y's. In some cases, the instrument in question might not contain responses to *items* as such. Readers of essays, for example, might produce ratings per essay. In these cases, your data analyst will help you find the best solution for completing the table.

If you have only *two* observers and their ratings will be based on just a few specific criteria rather than demand complicated decisions, then you can probably compute interrater reliability from the table by means of a *correlation.* A high correlation (roughly .70 or above) shows that the measurement method is sufficiently reliable. Lower correlations indicate that the observers or reports do not agree about what they are reporting and you should be correspondingly skeptical about the data you receive.

Some authors have nominated a correlation-like statistic, Cohen's Kappa,[10] as a substitute for more standard correlation coefficients when calculating interrater reliabilities with data from ranks or ratings. Kappa is easy to calculate and interpret, but only if data have been entered into the equation properly. For this, once more, you will need a data analyst.

If you will use *more than two* observers or raters, *or* if your two raters will be required to make decisions using multiple criteria, *or* if they will record many different features of what they see, then it might be appropriate to estimate interrater reliability using analysis of variance (ANOVA) rather than a correlation.[11] Since the exact form of ANOVA you use will depend on your situation, and since the best way to perform the ANOVA is by computer, you should consult a data analyst to help you in this case.

Determining the Reliability of Tests
That You Construct Yourself

Determining the reliability of your own tests requires that you calculate a statistic such as a correlation that shows the relationship between different administrations of the instrument or among items on the instrument at a single administration.

TABLE 7
Data Display to Begin Calculating
Interrater Reliability

Instrument Items	Rater or Observer X	Rater or Observer Y
1		
2		
3		
4		
5		
6		
7		
etc.		

Calculating any correlation coefficient involves setting up the results from various administrations of instruments according to Table 8. You will notice that the columns are labeled X and Y. Column X refers to one administration of an instrument. Column Y refers to another. If you are calculating reliability, X is administration 1, Y is administration 2. (If you were calculating concurrent or predictive *validity*, then X would be the instrument that you were validating, and Y would be the instrument that you were using as a criterion.) Listed down the left-hand column are respondents' names. While you need not refer to people by name, the left-hand column should contain some listing of individuals to whom both administrations have been given. In order to array data for calculating a correlation, simply list the scores on the various measures attained by each person. Then use a standard statistics text to choose the correlation coefficient appropriate to the type of data the tests have generated.[12]

If you plan to calculate a reliability coefficient for *your own* tests, the following pointers, based on previous experience of test developers, will help you increase the likelihood of obtaining a high coefficient.

Suggestion 1. Beware that calculating a correlation coefficient may give you an inaccurate estimate of reliability

Determining a reliability coefficient for a test usually means calculating a correlation between its two administrations. The size of correlation is affected by the *variability* of the *scores* obtained. In other words, if a test is reliable, then the results from administration A and administration B

TABLE 8
Data Display to Begin Calculating
a Correlation Coefficient

Names	X	Y
Evans, E. Handler, H. Kendall, K. Lee, L. Norris, N. Olsen, O. Ryan, R. Sanford, S. Turner, T. Weston, W.		

are most likely to show a high correlation *if both administrations have produced a wide range of values.* This is so because all measurement is subject to error; and if there is very little difference among the scores of different people (i.e., low variability), then only a little error will be required to render a person's standing at administration B different from his or her standing at administration A.

In computing reliabilities of long, general, usually norm-referenced tests, you can promote high score variability by (1) including a wide range of different skill levels among the people cooperating in the reliability study, (2) using a large sample, and (3) manipulating some characteristic of the test. These strategies render *correlation* an appropriate reliability check with long tests of general skills or aptitudes. In the case of criterion-referenced tests, however, low score variability can be common. This is because any one criterion-referenced test is usually short, allowing a range of scores across perhaps only five items. What is more, such tests are constructed so that everyone who has the skill in question will receive high scores. People will either score high and pass them or fail them outright. For this reason, most writers on the subject of the technical quality of criterion-referenced tests recommend checks on the reliability of the *decisions* made about people using these tests rather than scores received. A reliability study of this sort would require setting up the results of two test administrations as in Table 9. One of several statistical techniques can then be used to determine whether the pass-fail pattern shown in the table could have occurred by chance.[13] If a

TABLE 9
Number of Persons Passing and Failing
a Criterion-Referenced Test on
Two Administrations

| | | ADMINISTRATION 1 | |
		Passed	Failed
ADMINIS-TRATION 2	Passed	45	14
	Failed	4	56

fair degree of relationship appears to exist between decisions based on the two administrations, then the test is reliable.

Suggestion 2. Conduct an item analysis as a means of increasing test reliability

The purpose of an item analysis is to point out items that tend to reduce the scores of respondents who score high or to raise the scores of respondents who score low. In other words, item analysis helps you to find items that, for one reason or another, are inappropriate to the test, so that they can be removed or changed. Poor items lower reliability by reducing score variability or the homogeneity of criterion-referenced test items. Because of this, of course, they also make the test less valid.

Statistical techniques of item analysis are described in most measurement texts for making comparisons between how respondents performed on individual items and how they scored on the instrument as a whole. You can perform an *informal* item analysis by the method illustrated in this example:

Example. The first draft of a general science achievement test containing 65 items has been administered to 80 students. Twenty high and 20 low scorers, that is, the top and bottom 25 percent of the 80 students, have been identified. The completed instruments from these 40 students are examined, and the responses to each item are summarized in Table 10. The table's columns name the possible scores for each item—in this case, pass or fail. The rows list the items. By placing in one pile the responses of high scorers (those whose total score fell in the upper 25% range) and in a second pile the responses of low scorers (those whose total score fell in the lower 25% range), the evaluator can make a quick tally of how the people in each of the groups scored on each item. This is what the table tells you:

TABLE 10
Tallies of Pass/Fail Patterns Per Item for the 20 Highest and Lowest Scorers on a General Science Test

Item No.	20 highest scorers' scoring pattern		20 lowest scorers' scoring pattern	
	Pass	Fail	Pass	Fail
1	///	卌 卌 卌 //	卌 卌 卌 卌	
2	卌 卌 卌 //	///	卌 卌 卌 ///	//
3	卌 卌 卌	卌	卌 /	卌 卌 ////
4	卌 卌 卌 ///	//	///	卌 卌 //

etc.
to 65

- If the test will be used to *select* students for a program you may want to shorten the test a great deal while retaining those items that most high scorers get right and that most low scorers tend to fail. In this case, you would discard items 1, 2, and 3 but retain item 4.
- If this is a criterion-referenced test, then you will want to look at item 1 closely to find out what went wrong. Can you see by examining the item why the high scorers on this test usually got the first item wrong and why the low scorers passed it? The second item appears to have been easy for all but a few students. Was the objective measured by this item an easy objective, was there a "giveaway" element to the item, or was the objective just so well taught that the results reflect effective instruction? You may have to interview some students whose performance on particular items is puzzling. Thus for measuring performance via a criterion-referenced test, the only item that is clearly "misfiring" is item 1. Which of the other items to retain for a CRT should be based on factors other than their power to discriminate high from low scorers?

Suggestion 3. Try to build the reliability and validity tests into your assessment plan so that they present minimal inconvenience to yourself and the program staff

If you have little reason to doubt the validity of the test, you can use the results from its "official administration" as part of a reliability or validity check. For instance, you might randomly choose a group of respondents and administer the test to this group twice—once, at the time of data collection, and perhaps three weeks before or after. The calculation of relationship for the random group between these two administrations is your check on reliability. A *validity* study could proceed in much the same way. The criterion against which your test is to be validated—another test, classroom performance, or teacher rating—could be administered to a sample of your respondents at roughly the same time as the administration of your test.

Reliability and the Measurement of Complex Performance

Some guidance about what constitutes high and low reliability in instruments you choose to use is in order, since repeated reference is made to them in this chapter. Reliability coefficients of .70 or above are usually considered respectable, regardless of the type of reliability calculated or the method of calculation used; and coefficients of .90 and above are not unusual for standardized achievement tests. In the case of tests aimed at assessing performance of higher-order or complex skills—such as problem solving, creativity, good writing, and various measures of on the job performance—reliability coefficients tend to be somewhat lower. This is because these measures often rely upon the scoring of real life performances; and unless the scoring method has been elaborately detailed and used with highly trained scorers and observers, reliability tends to suffer. While reliability coefficients of .70 are certainly desirable among such measures, lower coefficients are sometimes tolerated, although this could affect the confidence with which you can make decisions based on test results.

If only tests of doubtful reliability are available to you, consider the amount of time and effort it takes to administer, score, and interpret them, and the amount of inconvenience they cause for respondents. The more resources an instrument demands, the more you should hesitate to use it if its reliability is low. A less reliable test is less likely to reveal the *real difference* that you hope the program makes. On the other hand, if you have the necessary time, and you are not overly burdening the respondents, an additional measure might provide you with good hunches about program effects.

Low reliability poses a particular kind of disadvantage for program evaluation. You are using the instruments, after all, to monitor the effectiveness of a program. Typically this means comparing one group mean with another, say two groups receiving different programs, or the same program at different times. Because the error associated with low reliability is random, that error will tend to affect both administrations. It will *not* systematically bias the results in favor for or against either administration. What low reliability will do is blur the difference between the two group measures. It is as if the instrument were trying to give you a message about program effectiveness, but its low reliability introduced static into your reception. If the message gets through anyway, then the low reliability poses no problem. The difficulty is that when the reliability is low, you may not get the message at all. Your statistical test is more likely to register "no significant difference" as a result of increased variance due to error (as opposed to good variance due to the construct) on each measure. And if this is the result of your study, apologizing for the low reliability of the instrument is likely to sound like Monday-morning quarterbacking—a poor substitute for favorable results.

The need for high test reliability in *program* studies is, however, less crucial than when you are making decisions about individuals. The reason is that statistical bases for *selecting* individuals according to relative standing on a measure are directly related to reliability. In such a situation, you are primarily concerned with purely statistically based predictive validity. In program evaluation, your primary concern is with construct validity and content validity. These, as you have seen, can be demonstrated by methods other than correlations.

Notes

1. Writers on the topic of criterion-referenced tests usually talk about constructs in terms of one or more behavior domains, emphasizing that these tests sample from and predict observable performances. For a highly readable discussion of *domain definition*, as well as issues surrounding the reliability and validity of these measures, see Popham (1970).

2. Correlations are mentioned often throughout this chapter. Correlation refers to the strength of the relationship between two measures. A high *positive* correlation means that people scoring high on one measure also score high on the other. A *negative* correlation also shows a strong relationship but in the opposite direction. *No* correlation means that knowing an individual's score on one measure does not educate your guess about their scores on the other. Correlations are usually expressed by a *correlation coefficient*, a decimal between −1 and +1, calculated from people's scores on the two different measures. Since there are several different correlation coefficients, each depending on the type of instruments being used, discussion of how to perform correlations to determine validity or reliability is outside the scope of this book. The

various correlation coefficients are discussed in most statistics texts, however. You might also refer to Fitz-Gibbon and Morris (1978).

3. An exception to this can be found in Huynh (1977).

4. For a test addressed to a large general subject area, this construct collage will bear a strong resemblance to the test plan or content/process matrix. They are alternative ways of mapping the territory covered by the test.

5. Popham (1978, p. 155) prefers to call this *descriptive* validity. He suggests two methods for defending validity of criterion-referenced measures: judgments by raters of item homogeneity, and criterion-group tryouts.

6. For an in-depth discussion of methods for systematically breaking down constructs in preparation for testing, see Guttman (1970).

7. This is usually done by developing and trying out a large pool of items and then assigning half to each test form.

8. It is not useful to calculate split-half reliability for criterion-referenced tests that have only five or so items.

9. This necessity, if you think about it, makes split-half reliability similar to alternate-form reliability with both forms administered at the same time.

10. Description of Cohen's Kappa can be found in Cohen (1960). Also see Fleiss (1973).

11. Analysis of variance is discussed briefly in Fitz-Gibbon and Morris (1987b).

12. See, for example, Fitz-Gibbon and Morris (1987a).

13. A phi coefficient or a chi-square test come first to mind, but these might give too low an estimate of relationship. Some statisticians recommend *Cohen's kappa* for determining relationships among measures placing scores into categories. See note 10 for this reference. It should be noted that a criterion-referenced test can place scores into *more than two* categories; that is, Table 9 could have had additional cells—for instance, Pass/Needs Remediation/Fail. Cohen's kappa handles these situations as well.

For Further Reading

American Psychological Association. Educational Research Association, National Council on Measurement in Education. (1974). *Standards for educational and psychological tests.* Washington, DC: Author.

Anastasi, A. (1968). *Psychological testing.* New York: Macmillan.

Citron, C. H. (1983). Courts provide insight on content validity requirements. *Educational Measurement: Issues and Practice, 2,* 6-7.

Cronbach, L. J. (1970) Test validation. In R. L. Thorndike (Ed.), *Educational measurement.* Washington, DC: American Council on Education.

Fitz-Gibbon, C. T., & Morris, L. L. (1987) *How to analyze data.* Newbury Park, CA: Sage.

Hambleton, R. K., et al. (1978). Criterion-referenced testing and measurement: A review of technical issues and developments. *Review of Educational Research, 48*(1), 1-47.

Jolly, S. J., & Gromenz, G. W. (1984). Customizing a norm-referenced achievement test to achieve curricular validity: A case study. *Educational Measurement: Issues and Practices, 3,* 16-18.

Mehrens, W. A., & Lehmann, I. J. (1984). *Measurement and evaluation in education and psychology.* New York: Holt, Rinehart & Winston.

Poggio, J. P., Glasnapp, D. R., Miller, M. D., Tollefson, N., & Burry, J. A. (1986) Strategies for validating teacher certification tests. *Educational Measurement: Issues and Practices, 5*, 18-25.

Popham, W. J. (1981). *Modern educational measurement.* Englewood Cliffs, NJ: Prentice-Hall.

Chapter 6
Using Performance Test Data

Once the performance test you have selected or designed has been administered, you face the task of organizing the information and extracting what is relevant for your use. You must use the data to judge how well the program—or an experimental treatment if you are conducting a short experiment—has achieved its intended objectives. However, you might also want to characterize the program or its participants in any number of other ways, possibly calculating correlations to show relationships among performance and respondent or program characteristics. The suggestions provided by this chapter will help you to work with the performance scores you obtain and to complete the following tasks:

- recording data from performance measures that you have constructed;
- preparing what you will report about the program by calculating statistics and displaying results.

Recording Data from Performance Measures That You Have Constructed

Purchased tests often come with scoring services. You, of course, will have to arrange your own scoring for tests constructed by yourself or the program staff. If your test scoring task is a large one, you might be able to lease or purchase a scoring machine. Sales representatives from data processing companies can provide you with sales and rental information.

Before you can interpret the scores, you may have to record the data from the tests onto a data summary sheet. Some performance tests yield a single number—either the total number of items answered correctly or the total number of points earned. In some situations, however, you will want to know how well respondents performed on *subtests* or on *groups of items* measuring the same objectives. To score separately subparts of a test, you will need to record data on a summary sheet like the one in Figure 8, which shows a commonsense way of tallying respondents'

	Objective 1 *Items:* M=4/5 *1,6,12,15,19*		Objective 2 *Items:* M=3/3 *3, 9,10*		Objective 3 *Items:* M=5/6 *5,14,18* points	
Student	Score	M	Score	M	Score	M
Barker, B.	4	+	2	0	3	0
Collins, C.	3	0	0	0	5	+
Dawson, D.	5	+	2	0	6	+
Drew, N.	1	0	2	0	4	0
Engel, E.	5	+	2	0	4	0

Figure 8. Data summary sheet for scoring an achievement test objective-by-objective. See text for explanation.

correct responses by objective.

Respondent names are listed down the left-hand side of the data summary sheet. Objectives are listed across horizontally, at the head of columns, identified by number. Each objective has two columns. In the first column, you record the raw score on the items addressing the objective. The M at the head of the second column stands for mastery; criteria for mastery of each objective are listed as, for instance, M = 4/5—a fraction in the cell naming the objective. In the second column, you record a + or a zero, depending on whether the raw score has met the mastery criterion. Respondents Dawson and Engle got all the items correct for Objective 1; respondent Barker had one wrong answer, but the criterion requiring that four out of five answers be correct determined that a + be put in Barker's M column also. You will notice that the method for recording scores for Objective 1 "loses" information about the respondents' success with individual items. Most analyses you perform, however, will not require item-by-item information.

No respondent achieved the three out of three mastery criterion for Objective 2.

Items for Objective 3 are scored somewhat differently. For each of these items, a respondent can receive either *one or two points*. Though the subtest has three items, six points can be earned. The score column for Objective 3 contains the total number of points earned over the three items.

Graph paper, or the kind of paper used for computer programming, is useful for constructing these data summary sheets even when the data are to be processed by hand rather than by computer.

Summary Sheets for Computer Analyses

If a computer analyzes your data, then your data summary task will involve coding responses or arranging response sheets in preparation for keypunching.[1] *Coding sheets* for setting up a file of your results for the computer can either follow the format of the data summary sheet in Figure 8 or record each respondent's scores item by item. The latter is probably wiser since you could decide later to use item-by-item information—perhaps to correlate test scores with some other respondent characteristic or to conduct item analyses, as described on pages 117 and 118.

When achievement data are keypunched, entries for each examinee will become a separate card or a span of tape. The standard card has 80 columns, so you can fit up to 80 pieces of single-digit information about each respondent on a card. The meaning of the digit in each column of the card is defined by a *codebook* written by the data analyst. Data coding is accomplished by punching holes over the numbers in the 80 card columns. When there is information to fill more than 80 columns, a second card is simply inserted behind the first card in the data deck or by coding continuously on tape.

Mechanical data processing, including computer analyses of data and perhaps even *machine scoring of test answer forms*, will affect the form of your data summary sheet or perhaps even make it unnecessary to have one. Since computer analyses and machine-scored testing are easily accessible, you can perhaps conserve your own time by investigating these services. If you find that mechanical data processing fits your time constraints and budget, then your data summary sheet will need to conform to the machine's requirements. You might even find that the respondent's answer sheet, if formatted properly, can be *read* and *scored* by a machine or that you can use a machine-scorable answer sheet. You might also adopt a general purpose machine-scorable answer sheet, like the one in Figure 9, to save time for everyone who must process test scores rapidly and accurately. In any case, if you plan to use machine scoring or computer data processing, discuss the format and content of your tests with your data analyst before you produce them en masse.

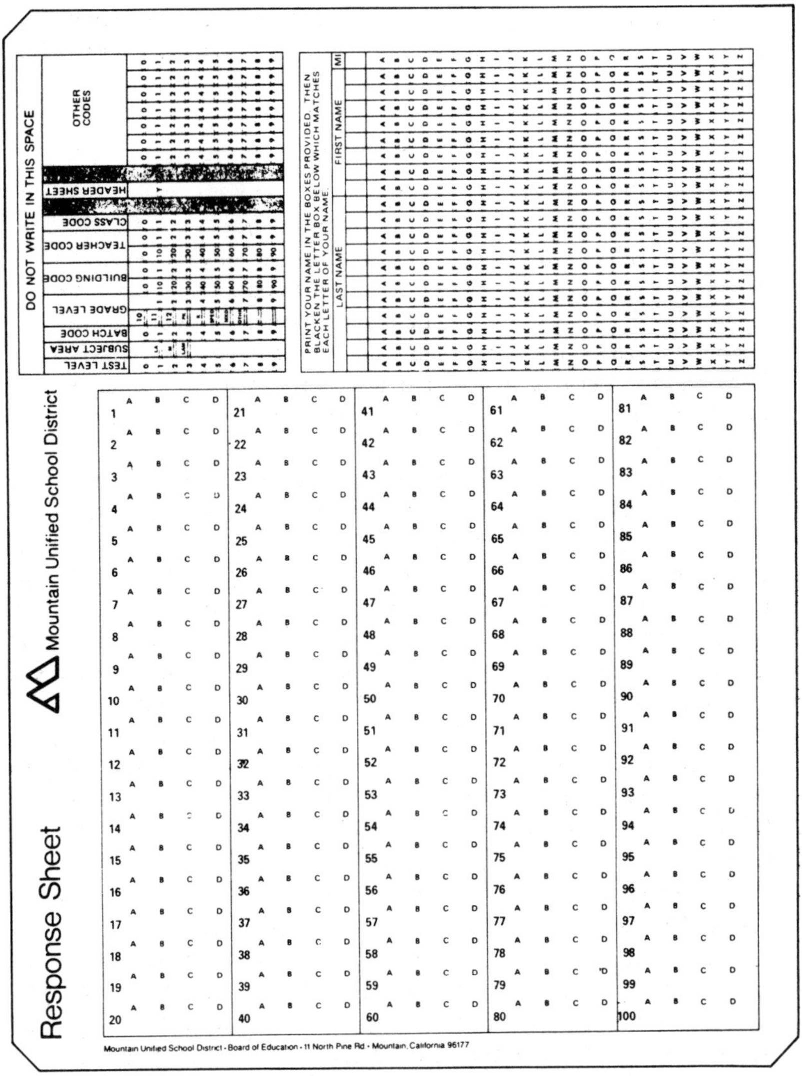

Figure 9. General purpose machine scorable answer sheet

What to Report About the Program

Norm- and criterion-referenced tests produce myriad types of scores. Depending on what your audience wants to know, these scores can be used to perform many analyses. It is likely that the questions your evaluation is supposed to answer—those that have guided you all along—will decide what sorts of scores you collect and how you analyze and report them.

To suggest what you might do with performance test scores, this section describes the types of scores that tests produce and explains some of the analyses that can be performed to answer different evaluation questions.

Types of Scores

Before you attempt to interpret a set of scores, you should understand what they can and cannot tell you. You may encounter three major types of performance test scores:

- raw scores
- scores from criterion-referenced tests
- scores from norm-referenced tests

Raw scores

Raw scores are aptly named. They are the first summary numbers you obtain when you score tests. They are computed prior to any conversion process introducing norms or performance standards. The most common raw score is the total number of items answered correctly. With tests that assign a different number of points to different items, the raw score is the total number of points earned. On timed tests, the raw score could be the speed with which the task has been done. Number of errors is another form of raw score. At times when speed and accuracy are important, such as in typing, the raw score usually includes both a determination of time elapsed and number of errors.

Whether you construct the test yourself or use a published one, you have the option of reporting raw scores and using them in your data analyses. Even if tests are to be sent away for scoring, you may want to score them yourself in order to get the raw score data early. Some test publishers provide scoring stencils so that you can calculate a quick score before the tests are sent away. You may also need to compute raw scores yourself if you want results from *groups of items* on the test rather than the entire test. Often the computer printout you receive from the publisher will report individual raw scores and averages along with corresponding percentiles and other norm scores.

Though raw scores out of context are hard to interpret, they are not meaningless. Raw scores are directly interpretable, for instance, in domain-referenced tests where you can clearly describe what it is the test measures. Raw scores, because they are most directly derived from the test, are, in addition, the appropriate numbers to be used when calculating statistics. T-tests, for instance, or analyses of variance, computed to determine whether there is a difference in average scores between a program and control group, should be based on average raw scores, *not on converted scores.*

Criterion-referenced scores

Criterion-referenced scores are, of course, the scores obtained from criterion-referenced tests. An important feature of many of these tests is the establishment of a criterion-level or cutoff score that determines passing, mastery, or acceptable performance. Because criterion-referenced tests are concerned with mastery, the score for any individual student is expressed usually as a *dichotomous*, either-or judgment: The student has *passed* the test, exceeding the cutoff score, or has *failed* to do so. Occasionally, criterion tests will categorize performance into three or more levels, such as poor performance, remediable performance, and passing.

There is a growing literature on the subject of establishing performance standards of cutoff scores (see, e.g., Hambleton, Swaminathan, Algina, & Coulson, 1978; Swaminathan, Hambleton, & Algina, 1974). The question of how many correct, or what level of performance should constitute mastery, or superior as opposed to mediocre performance, is a popular one. The issue is particularly pressing because of the legal as well as educational issues associated with competency testing.[2]

Since an acceptable *program* must be effective with *groups* of students, you will usually need to present group results from criterion-referenced tests. When dealing with individuals, a criterion test gives you information only about success or failure at passing a particular objective, or meeting a certain proficiency standard. Quite a few methods are available for summarizing this pass-fail information in order to describe the performance of *groups*. The different approaches you can take with these summaries are discussed in a later section of the chapter beginning on page 131.

Norm-referenced scores

The norm scores available to you will nearly always reflect the performance of *individual students* as compared with other individuals.

Norms may also be provided for classrooms, schools, or districts. Norm scores are often gathered as a result of a mandated statewide or districtwide testing program.

When norm-referenced tests are scored, the raw scores for each student or groups of students are converted into a norm-referenced percentile, stanine, or grade equivalent—a *standard* score that reflects the position of the raw score in comparison with members of the norm or standard *group*. Norm scores will be useful when you need to estimate for your audience how closely the performance of program participants matches that of a national or local norm group.

The most common norm scores are described in manuals accompanying published tests. Unlike statewide or local norms that reflect the rank of your school or students with respect to others in the same locality or of a similar background, norm score conversions provided by a test publisher are usually based on performance of some external norm or reference group. This external group is the set of students who were selected and tested by the test producers during the test's actual development—that is, during a certain month of a certain year, possibly some years ago. The reference or norm group is also called the standardization group. In fairness to the program you are evaluating, you want the standardization group to be representative of the students and grade levels it concerns.

The most common norm-referenced scores are these:

- *percentiles* (also called centiles and percentile ranks), which show approximately what percentage of students scored lower than a given raw score;
- z-scores, T-scores, and other *linear standard scores*, which tell you how many standard deviations above or below the mean a given raw score has fallen;
- T-scaled scores, stanines, and other *normalized standard scores*, which tell you *approximately* how many standard deviations above or below the mean a given raw score is, but are actually based on percentiles;
- *Grade-equivalent scores*, which attempt to tell you what grade level—in years and months—typically corresponds to a given raw score. Because of the questionable manner in which they are derived, and because they are easily misinterpreted, grade equivalents should *not* be used as indicators of program performance.

Several sources containing detailed descriptions of the construction, scoring, and interpretation of norm-referenced tests are listed in "For Further Reading" at the end of this chapter.

Please note a common error that is made when norm scores are used to describe group performance: The mean of the individual norm scores from a group—say, a school—does *not* equal the norm score of the mean of the group. If, for instance, you administered the Comprehensive Test of Basic Abilities (CTBA) and calculated an average of the percentile scores of individual students, this number would *not* reflect the percentile of the school's average when compared with other schools. If the average percentile of the students in your school is 67, this does not mean that the school itself stands at the 67th percentile among schools.

In order to provide you with this information, the publisher would have to calculate the average raw score for each school using the CTBA and then compute a percentile ranking of *schools.* Few test developers do this. When the median percentile rank achieved by students in the school is a meaningful and useful number to report, be careful to inform your audiences that it might not accurately reflect the *school's* standing. Some state assessment programs do report school percentile rankings. This is usually the case when the state itself develops, administers, and norms the test. In this situation, the percentile that is reported reflects the actual standing of the school with respect to the other schools in the state.

Using Performance Test Scores to Answer Common Evaluation Questions

This section discusses five questions that program evaluators usually find themselves answering or attempting to answer, namely:

- Which participants should be placed in the program?
- How do the scores of program participants compare with those of a control or comparison group?
- How do scores compare with past performance?
- To what extent have program objectives been obtained?
- Are performance test results related to participant characteristics or program variations?

In discussing the use of performance scores in answering these questions, advice is given concerning the appropriate type or types of scores to use—criterion-referenced, norm-referenced, or raw scores. Some suggestions are also given with respect to reporting scores and using graphs and tables.

Question 1: Which participants should be placed in the program?

It might occur that a funding agency has already prescribed the tests and cutoff scores to be used for selecting participants to take part in a program. In this case, of course, the question of placement has been answered for you. In other situations, however, you may have to make such determinations yourself. Where the decision is yours, beware of placing too much emphasis on a single test score. An individual's score, always remember, is only an *imperfect* estimate of his or her knowledge, skill, or ability, an estimate that is more accurate for some than for others. Because individual test scores can be subject to significant error, you will want to guard against their misuse. Considering a variety of indicators in addition to test scores is one way to avoid unfair or otherwise faulty decisions.

How you decide which individuals should be in the program will depend on whether the program is intended for an "extreme" group— high or low performance—or whether the program participants are supposed to be representative of individuals who span a range of abilities.

In selecting an extreme group to receive, for example, remedial instruction in math, you might opt to use either norm- or criterion-referenced tests. Your choice of test will be based on whether you want to select *a fixed number of participants who are most in need* or whether you wish to identify *everyone in need* as determined by a cutoff score. Say, for example, that there is room in a remedial class for only 20 participants; then you might simply select the 20 participants with the lowest scores. In this case, a norm-referenced test will probably serve you better because it draws fine distinctions among people with extreme strengths and deficiencies. Norm-referenced aptitude tests should also be considered if general ability is relevant to whether participants are placed in a program.

If, on the other hand, the program intends to address a particular set of skills that all individuals are expected to learn, then criterion-referenced measures, with appropriate recommendations for cutoff scores, should help you identify every person who needs this instruction.

In some situations, you might want to select a program group that is *representative* of a large group of potential participants. This might occur, for instance, if you want to try out a pilot program with a small group before adopting it districtwide. To select a representative group, you should *graph raw scores* from whatever measure you deem most relevant for selecting program participants. Then, looking at the graph, see whether scores divide themselves into clusters or whether they form a smooth, almost continuous curve. Clusters of scores provide you with natural cutoff points; If the graph shows a smooth distribution, you will have to draw more arbitrary cutoff points between groups. After this, sample from each group or cluster so that the total program group contains high, middle, and low scorers in the same proportions as the larger group from which they are selected.

In some rare instances, you may be interested in choosing participants for a program who have a specific skill deficiency, for instance, who cannot swim or who cannot take apart a carburetor. In these situations you will, of course, construct a criterion test that gives respondents a chance to display the particular skill.

Question 2: How do the scores of program participants compare with those of a control or comparison group?

Your evaluation might use a control or comparison group design to allow you to estimate how program participants might have performed had they not taken part in the program. In such a case, you will want to compare performance results from the two groups.

If the outcome measure is a norm-referenced test, then the best determiner of comparative outcomes is a test for the statistical significance of differences in the average *raw scores* from the groups on the testing question. If just *two* groups are being compared, then a t-test for the difference between means is probably the appropriate statistic. If more than two are being compared, then an analysis of variance should be performed. These techniques are described in most statistics books.[3]

Table 11 shows an example of how to report results of an evaluation using a pretest-posttest design with a true control group. The table for the non-equivalent control group design is identical. Table 11 displays mean raw scores for each program, the standard deviation associated with each mean, and the t-test of the difference between means for both the pretest and posttest. Note in this example that the pretest was a norm-referenced *ability* test and the posttest was a norm-referenced *performance* test. The t-test for the difference between pretest scores was not significant. This is indicated by the *absence* of an asterisk. This means that on the pretest the two groups were more or less equivalent. If the difference between ability test scores on the pretest had been significant, then the evaluator would have been in trouble—the reason for using such a design is to show a difference on the posttest scores

TABLE 11
Pretest and Posttest Results for Program Alpha
and Program Beta Participants

	N	Pretest (ability)			Posttest (performance)		
		Mean	SD	t-test of diff.	Mean	SD	t-test of diff.
Alpha	8	24.00	7.25	0.25	30.30	5.10	4.16*
Beta	14	24.86	7.12		15.80	8.60	

*Statistically significant at the .05 level.

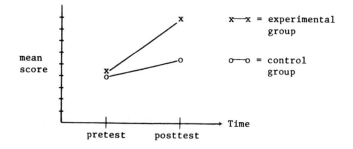

Figure 10. Mean scores of the experimental group
and control group on the pretest and posttest

between two groups that had initially performed similarly. Having established that the groups were equivalent to begin with, one then looks at results *after* the program, again by performing a t-test on raw score means. The example shows a large difference between the posttest means. Not surprisingly, the t-test shows the difference to be significant, that is, bigger than could have been expected to occur by chance. For the example shown in Table 11, the evaluator can report this:

> As was expected because of the use of random selection, the Alpha program and Beta control participants were initially equivalent on the ability measure used as the pretest. After the program, however, the mean posttest score of the Alpha program participants was significantly higher than the mean score of the Beta control group. This gain by Alpha participants can be attributed to their participation in the program.

In addition to a table, raw scores results from pretest and posttest can be displayed on a graph. Graphic representation is recommended because graphs are quickly understood and interpreted. In addition, graphs are almost always preferable when presenting results to a live audience. If the pre- and posttest were the *same* test or an equivalent or parallel form of the same test, then using this kind of graph will always be appropriate.

If the pretest was *different* from the posttest—such as the ability test in Table 11—then display the posttest scores only. This is the simplest method of display and is acceptable if there was no significant difference between pretest scores:

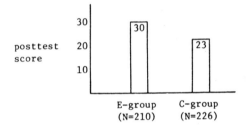

Figure 11. Mean posttest scores of the E-group and C-group

When interpreting results from a control group design study, remember the critical question:

Was the posttest mean for one group significantly different from the posttest mean for the other group?

It is not good procedure to test the difference between *group gains* from pretest to posttest. For statistical reasons, comparing gains usually penalizes the group whose pretest score was higher. Therefore, compare the scores between groups on either the pretest or posttest, *not* the differences in score *gains* from pretest to posttest.

When deciding whether observed differences in mean scores are *educationally* significant, confidence limits usually are a more useful statistic than the t-test. While a t-test of significance tells you whether the difference you have found is more than a chance difference, confidence limits give you an estimate of the range of differences you would find between experimental and control groups were you to repeat the study again and again. This range not only gives you an idea of how big the actual difference between the groups might be; it also permits a quick check on whether the difference obtained is significant.

If the mean posttest raw score is higher for the program group than for the control group, but not significantly different statistically, you might ask a data analyst to try a more powerful statistical test such as analysis of variance or analysis of covariance, discussed in most basic statistics texts.

If a battery of criterion-referenced tests has been used to determine the performance of program and control group students, you can use a *total raw score* equal to the number of items correct on the whole battery to perform an analysis exactly the same as the one described here for norm-referenced tests. If, however, some objectives are more important than others, or if you wish to make interpretations of the test on an objective-by-objective basis, then statistical analyses of total scores will not give appropriate information for comparing the programs. What to do instead is discussed under Question 4 below.

Question 3: How do scores compare with past performance?

In the absence of a control group, you may wish to use test results to express the results from a *time series design* or to document a change in the program group's performance *from pretest to posttest*. Such comparisons can take one of two forms. First, you can compare the scores of a group with *their own previous scores* on the same measure or its equivalent form. A formative evaluator monitoring progress, for instance, might give program participants the same test periodically throughout the course of the program. A summative evaluator might decide to look at the program group's performance at last year's administration of the outcome measure—or perhaps over the last two years. In both cases, the measurement plan is said to be *longitudinal*. Pretest-posttest designs are always longitudinal.

In contrast, you might find it useful to employ a *successive groups design*, comparing current test results with past scores from *different* participants who were then at the same developmental or grade level as those in the program. The successive groups design is often used in summative evaluations where a particular test is annually administered to a particular grade level.

When comparing changes in mean scores over time, whether with successive groups or longitudinally, you should use *raw scores* for both graphing and analysis.

Whether you choose to administer the *same* test over and again or to use equivalent forms is up to you. When using longitudinal and pretest-posttest designs, some evaluators prefer to administer *different* tests at each occasion to ensure against memory effects—learning of specific test items rather than generalized learning related to the objectives measured by the test. In order to eliminate item-specific memory effects, many test developers have created *parallel* or *alternate forms* of a test—with varying degrees of success.

You can check the degree of parallelism in tests you use in different ways. As evidence that different forms of a test will be parallel, *criterion-referenced test* developers rely on the care with which objectives have been described and the manner in which items have been sampled from the pool of potential items. You will have to use your judgment concerning a publisher's claims in this regard. You will find it easier to accept such descriptive evidence when dealing with tests of simple tasks, such as word-attack skills or arithmetic computation, than with tests of reading comprehension or other complex skills where specification of item types is looser. *Norm-referenced test* developers, on the other hand, are expected to provide in the test manual statistical evidence that two test forms are equivalent. Two types of data are usually reported— norms and correlations. When separate norms have been computed for each form, a glance at the relative positions of means or medians will tell you whether the group tested did better on one form than the other, and if so, how much better. Correlation of each student's performance on both forms will yield an *alternative form reliability coefficient*. Coefficients of .90 or greater are good evidence of equivalence.

If you are satisfied with evidence of equivalence of forms—and if you feel your audience will be as well—then you can compare pretest-posttest and time series scores as if participants were being retested with the same instrument. Where evidence of equivalence is *weak*, build insurance against non-parallelism into your evaluation: The first time you administer the test, randomly divide program participants in two and give, say, Form A to one half and Form B to the other, keeping a record of which participants took which form of the test. Then when it is time to posttest or retest, give Form B to those who had taken Form A, and vice versa. In this way, you will prevent any small differences between the forms from affecting your comparison of results on different occasions or for different groups. Effects from an easier form will wash out in the *group* data.

Reporting time series scores from norm-referenced tests. Figures 12 and 13 describe graphs for reporting results of longitudinal and successive time series measures. Figure 12 shows the results of two subtests of a norm-referenced test—language arts and math computation—administered by a formative evaluator to samples of students six times over the course of a 7th-grade language arts program. The program was initiated during the 14th week of school. You will notice that the raw scores of students on both subtests rise over the course of the school year. The slope of the languages arts gain, however, begins to *steepen* after initiation of the program. This gives good evidence that the language arts program, and not changes in the general school environment or in the particular pool of students with whom the program was introduced, brought about the observed change in scores over time. Notice that the evaluator in this situation controlled for memory effects upon retesting by selecting *samples* of students at each testing occasion. This strategy works with as few as 30 or 40 students per site. Randomly pulling a few students to test rather than measuring everyone is also kind to your budget and to teacher morale.

The same graphing method works with a successive groups time series design. Figure 13 shows median percentile ranks[4] on language arts and math computation subtests at the end of a school year for successive groups of students. The same norm-referenced achievement test in this case has been administered six years in a row.[5]

Reporting pretest-posttest results from norm-referenced tests. You can report scores on standardized tests using a table like Table 12. Scores displayed in the table represent a situation in which the *same* test has been given as both a pre- and posttest. The t-test tests the significance of the difference between mean pre- and posttest raw scores. It is a t-test for matched groups.

When interpreting these results, remind your audience of the following:

(1) If the program lasted any length of time, a significant difference between a pre- and posttest would be nearly always expected anyway. Students do better on any particular test as they grow older and accumulate experience. However, you might find a situation such as that shown for Math, School C, in Table 12: no significant difference between pre- and posttest scores. In this case, someone should look into what has been going on in this school. Was there a testing error, or are the students really making no progress?

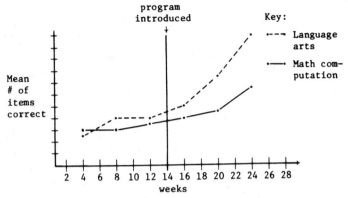

Figure 12. Time series trend graph showing mean raw scores from six administrations of language arts and math computation subtests of the Comprehensive Abilities Test, Form J, to samples of program students

(2) A studied decision should be made about how seriously scores from the norm-referenced test should be taken. This decision should be based on the following:

- awareness of how these tests are developed;
- assessment of the overlap in content of the test with the program being evaluated;
- description of the norm group with whom standard scores from the test are being compared.

Reporting criterion-referenced test scores over time. If your measure is a criterion-referenced test, then you will be able to use the time series graphs described *only if you can represent the results of the test by a single number.* Converting criterion-referenced test results into single numbers would demand this procedure:

- grouping objectives and then computing the mean number of students mastering each group;
- computing a raw score covering groups of objectives that are of about the same importance or deal with similar subject matter;
- using a single raw score from the entire battery if its objectives are of about equal importance.

These are discussed under Question 4.

If you have gone to the trouble, however, of collecting information

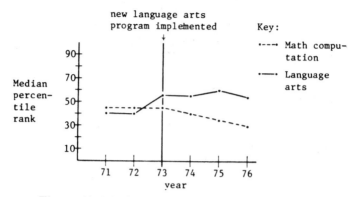

Figure 13. Median percentile ranks of successive seventh grades on language arts and math computation subtests of the Comprehensive Abilities Test administered over a six-year period

objective by objective, then you have much richer data about how the program students perform than can be communicated through a single number or graph. Your analysis should reflect this richness of information. An objective-by-objective presentation of criterion-referenced test results is discussed in detail in the next section.

Question 4: To what extent have program objectives been attained?

Results from criterion-referenced tests are usually analyzed in terms of objectives. This analysis, however, can take several forms. Four ways to answer Question 4 are described in this section:

- comparing results on each objective, either between groups receiving different programs or for the same group before and after instruction;
- comparing the number of objectives mastered per group;
- comparing amounts of time required by students to master objectives;
- reporting which objectives were mastered by many students and which were mastered by only a few *in a single group* and *at a single testing*.

Chapter 2 (pages 35-36) described a procedure for using a *norm-referenced test* to measure attainment of program objectives. As you can see from the procedure, objectives-based analysis of the results from most norm-referenced tests is extremely difficult. This is because of uncertainty about precisely which program objectives, if any, are measured by particular items and because the test may lack a sufficient

TABLE 12
**Mean Pretest and Mean Posttest Reading and Math Scores
for Schools in the XYZ Program**

Group	n[a]	Pretest	Posttest	t-test for difference between pre- and posttest
		Reading		
School A	401	59.4	64.3	3.8*
School B	720	50.2	70.5	12.2*
School C	364	40.9	60.2	4.5*
		Math		
School A	461	63.2	70.1	2.4*
School B	726	58.4	71.2	3.1*
School C	362	32.9	33.4	0.8

[a]Number present for both the pre- and posttests, and
therefore the students on whose scores the t-test was
calculated

*significant at .05 level

number of items for drawing conclusions about most objectives. Criterion-referenced tests, if they are well constructed, should not present these problems since they are *designed* to be interpreted in terms of objectives.

Comparing results on each objective, either between different groups or at different times. In general, it is not appropriate to perform tests of statistical significance for differences in scores for a single objective. The comparisons you make, therefore, will have to be informal, relying on discussion of tables and graphs. *Bar graphs* are especially useful for presenting data about achievement of an objective. Each bar can represent the *percentage of students passing* one objective if data have been reported per student, or the *mean percentage passing* if data have been aggregated by sites such as schools or classrooms. A glance at the graph reveals the program's strengths and weaknesses.

The example in Figure 14 shows results from the Compute-It and Think-Alot math programs for clusters of related objectives. Note that the passing rates for speed tests (Objectives Cluster A) were generally below 60% for both programs. It appears that the Compute-It program was more successful at teaching sets (Objectives Cluster B) and considerably more successful at teaching decimals (Objectives Cluster D). Looking at Cluster D, you might guess that the Think-Alot students did not receive instruction in the last five decimals objectives. Think-Alot appears to have produced better results, however, with fractions (Objectives Cluster C); perhaps more time was spent on that subject.

Results per objective could also be presented as *mean raw scores* on each objective for each group. If you wanted to see whether either program produced better *overall* results on the speed tests, for instance, you could average the raw score means for Objectives Cluster A.

When you discuss results portrayed as a mass of objective-by-objective comparisons, give foremost consideration to the *educational significance* of differences in performance. If the experimental group did better than the control group, how much better? If the differences are presented in terms of percentage of students passing, then what percentage difference would make you sit up and take notice? If you are averaging raw scores per objective, then what does the difference mean in terms of proportion of items right, and how much of a rise in that proportion would satisfy you?

Differences between the *pretest and posttest* performances of a single group can be shown objective by objective in a similar way. Table 13 and Figure 15 illustrate common methods for displaying changes in a single group's mastery of objectives from pretest to posttest. The table shows the *mean percentage of students in program classrooms* achieving 12 program objectives at pretest and posttest. Figure 15 graphically displays the same data. You can see from the figure that performance actually declined from pretest to posttest on objectives 1, 2, 9, 10, and 11, so the program is failing to teach some objectives. On the other hand, the number of students mastering objectives 5, 6, and 7 nearly doubled and rose to almost 70% for objective 5. If the program devoted much instructional time to these objectives, it may be sensible to credit the program with these improvements.

The quality of results from *a single group* can be more easily judged if they are compared against expected mastery levels set while the program was being planned. Where goals have been set regarding the percentage of students who should pass various objectives, you can graph results by grouping objectives, as in Figure 16. The graph shows that some objectives have a goal of 100% passing. In basic education, for instance, it might be decided that all students should be able to read pill taking instructions competently or know how to make change. For some objectives, and for a particular grade level, an 80% pass rate might be set

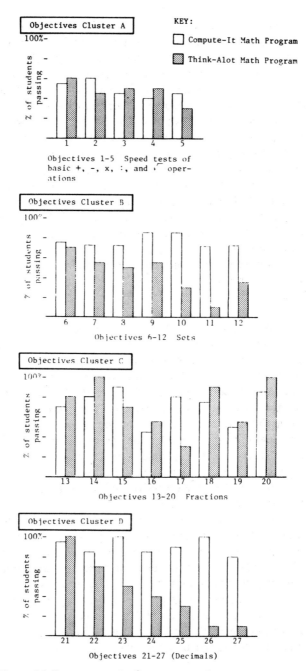

Figure 14. Posttest results from two math programs
for four clusters of objectives

TABLE 13

Mean Percent of Students in Program X Classrooms Achieving
the Twelve Objectives at Pretest and Posttest

Group	Objective # 1	2	3	4	5	6	7	8	9	10	11	12
Ninth grades (n=23)												
pretest	91	76	34	33	38	16	13	7	56	16	22	0
posttest	77	62	43	41	66	35	30	11	30	7	7	2

as the goal, and other objectives might be expected to be attained by only 20% of the students. Such might be the case with "enrichment" skills. You can see from Figure 16 that the goal of 100% passing was not reached for objectives 2 and 11; the goal of 80% passing was not achieved for objective 6; all the 20% objectives for enrichment were achieved; and three goals had already been achieved at the time of the pretest—objectives 4, 5, and 22.

If you wish to call attention to the percentage of students who moved from non-mastery to mastery on specific, highly critical program objectives, then you might consider including in your report a table such as Table 14. The table shows the pattern of student performance from pretest to posttest for important program objectives. The first row displays the percentage of students mastering the objectives over the course of the program. This row reflects to some degree the effectiveness of instruction. The second row lists the percentage of students for whom instruction on the objectives was unnecessary because they passed the pretest. Results in this column reflect little about the program except to show whether its objectives were appropriate for the student group in question. If too large a percentage of students appear in this row, then it could be argued that the program was a waste of time for a large proportion of the students. The third row shows the extent to which the program failed to come through for certain students—the ones who failed the posttest. Students are classified in this group whether or not they failed—or passed—the pretest. You might add a fourth row if you think that the program has done harm, leading to a decline in students' performance in the subject area; but this eventuality is usually unlikely.

Comparing the number of objectives mastered per group. For each student in a program or comparison group, you can obtain *a single score*

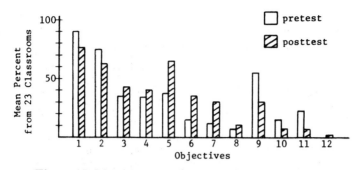

Figure 15. Mean percent of students in Program X classrooms achieving the twelve objectives at pretest and posttest

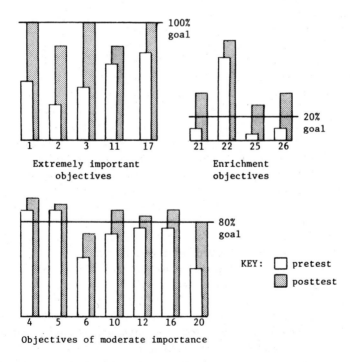

Figure 16. The achievement of program objectives showing different goals for the percent of students achieving the objectives

TABLE 14
Percent of Students Showing Three Different Patterns of Pre-Posttest Results on Important Program Objectives

Pattern of Test Results		1	2	Objective 4a	5b	7	9
I	Failed pretest/ Passed posttest	17					
II	Passed pretest/ Passed posttest	45					
III	Failed posttest	38					

that tells how many program objectives the student has mastered. These scores can then be aggregated to compute either the total or the mean number of objectives based by students in different groups, or by students in the same group from pretest to posttest. Reporting a single score per group has several advantages.

- It is a convenient way to summarize results, particularly if you are assessing the achievement of many objectives.
- If you wish to *compare* the performance of different groups, or pretest and posttest results from the same group, the difference between means can be tested for statistical significance in the same manner as more conventional total scores (see Table 12).
- Computing the mean number of objectives passed allows you to identify and characterize groups of students who fared particularly well or poorly on the posttest, and to produce gross measures of progress for groups that scored low, middle, and high on the pretest.

As you may have guessed, number-of-objectives-mastered scores also have disadvantages:

- They do not tell you *which* objectives were mastered and which were not.
- They treat all objectives as if they were of equal importance, though this frequently is not the case.
- Like all numbers based on mastery scores, they incorporate the arbitrariness that goes with setting cutoff points to define mastery.

Comparing amounts of time required by students to master objectives. Teaching toward mastery of objectives is based on the notion that any student can learn basic skills if given enough practice time. This naturally suggests a measure of how long it takes students to master critical program objectives. The *number of class hours* or *practice hours* it takes for, say, 50% of the students to attain *a particular set of objectives* could serve as a measure of program efficiency and therefore as a basis for program comparison.

Since the time measure must be based on mastery of *all* the objectives in a given set, the question of *which* objectives should compose this set should be settled beforehand. These could be some of the program's most critical objectives, a randomly chosen group of typical ones, a set representing particularly difficult-to-master skills, or perhaps a cluster of objectives that students failed on the pretest.

Time required to master objectives can also serve as an individual student score; it can be averaged and treated statistically like any such score. A time-to-mastery score is most suited to individualized learning programs and programs that use technological teaching aids such as language laboratories. In teaching situations where students do an indeterminate amount of out-of-class work, however, the amount of time spent on instruction or practice will be more difficult to determine. Also, unless tests of mastery can be mechanically or self-administered as soon as students are "ready," time measures will be limited by the fact that staff members are not continuously able to administer tests. If students have to wait to be tested, then time scores that a student obtains will become inaccurate.

Reporting which objectives were mastered by many students and which were mastered by only a few in a single group and at a single testing. Sometimes—particularly if your evaluation is formative—you will want to look at the results from a single test administration in order to locate objectives that students have failed to achieve. This information will give guidance to teachers and planners about which skills need attention. On the other hand, knowing which objectives *have* been attained by a large percentage of the students is also useful to formative evaluators; it will prevent teachers from giving superfluous instruction, and students from doing unnecessary work. Both formative and summative evaluators may want to investigate *why* the program has or has not been successful in producing certain kinds of learning. This may require taking a closer look at the program and its participants by investigating, for instance, student entry skills, student interests, teacher preparation, and the adequacy of program materials.

Analyzing student achievement of individual objectives requires first that you list program objectives and record beside each the number or percentage of students who have mastered it, based on test scores. These data can be compiled or graphed in various ways. The simplest way is a table that presents a single row of "percentage passing" for each objective, such as Table 15. Figure 17 shows a bar graph illustrating these same results. Notice how much easier it is to survey the results from the graph than from the table.

You might also want to present results of this kind of each classroom, grade level, or other grouping of program participants. Table 16 shows data per objective in terms of percentage of students passing in each *classroom*. Table 17 notes whether these percentages are greater or less than 80%, which was a goal the program sought to reach for each of the four objectives.

You can also *group* objectives based on the percentage of students mastering them. Table 18 divides student passing rates into four levels and classifies objectives accordingly.

In much of this section, it has been assumed that cutoff scores per objective are used to make *pass/fail* judgments only. However, there is nothing sacred about a two-way distinction, and you could identify three or more levels of performance per objective. Table 19 shows three-way outcomes for seven objectives on a unit test administered to 135 students. Not shown in the table are the criteria used for deciding what constitutes low, middle, and high performance. These criteria, chosen by the staff or the evaluation's audience, would be expressed as numbers of items per objective.

A table like this is useful for formative evaluation. It allows decisions about satisfactory performance to be made based on how many students scored at each level. Objectives needing remedial attention can be located quickly. In this case, a standard was set such that fewer than 27 students (20%) showing low performance and 81 or more of the students (60% or more) performing high on the objective would be considered satisfactory by the staff. They would not attempt to revise instruction for that objective unless there were other strong reasons—say, from interview data—to do so. On the other hand, if either condition were violated—27 or more in the low column *or* 80 or fewer in the high column—then the staff would not be satisfied, and an attempt would be made to locate the program deficiency and correct it.

Although the question of satisfaction in the table is always answered yes or no, the staff might also have expressed different degrees of satisfaction or dissatisfaction. While performance on both the first and second objectives is satisfactory, for instance, performance on the second is very satisfactory indeed. Similarly, performance on Objective 3 is more than unsatisfactory; it is dismal. Variation in the proportion of

TABLE 15
Mean Percent of Students in Program X
Achieving the Twelve Objectives at Pretest

Group	Objective #											
	1	2	3	4	5	6	7	8	9	10	11	12
Ninth grades (n=23)	91	76	34	33	38	16	13	7	56	16	22	0

students who have not achieved an objective may serve to focus greater staff attention on improving the program for some objectives than for others. It could also turn out that too many students in the low column will be more unacceptable than not enough students in the high column. Finally, primary attention may be given to revision for greater attainment on objectives that are considered by the staff to be prerequisite to success on subsequent objectives.

Question 5: How do performance test results relate to participant characteristics or program variations?

Answering this question means making statements of the following kinds: "Participants or programs with *this* pattern or degree of performance tended to have *that* characteristic." Participant characteristics that might be of interest include aptitude, socioeconomic background, rate of attendance, and level of "entering skills"—skills in the subject matter in question that participants possessed before entering the program. Relevant characteristics that vary within the program might be curriculum materials used, experience of teachers, class size, or amount of time allotted to particular kinds of instruction.

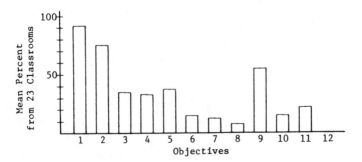

Figure 17. Mean percent of students in Program X achieving the twelve objectives at pretest

TABLE 16
Percentage of Students Passing the Objectives
in Each of the Classrooms

Classroom	Writes name	Knows colors	Reads lower-case letters	Reads capitals
1	99	85	83	70
2	98	87	82	60
3	98	80	78	65
4	90	78	60	69
5	95	82	72	79
6	99	90	87	80
7	92	85	60	65
8	98	82	90	76
9	99	87	84	70
10	99	87	81	62

TABLE 17
Objectives Passed by 80% or More
of the Students in the 10 Classrooms

Classroom	Writes name	Knows colors	Reads lower-case letters	Reads capitals
1	+	+	+	o
2	+	+	+	o
3	+	+	o	o
4	+	o	o	o
5	+	+	o	o
6	+	+	+	+
7	+	+	o	o
8	+	+	+	o
9	+	+	+	o
10	+	+	+	o

KEY: + = objective passed by 80% or more of the students
      o = objective passed by less than 80% of the students

One way to examine how the program affected people differentially—depending on ability levels, gender, attendance rates, or whatever—is *to compare results from different subgroups.* Comparing the performance of different groups might give you evidence that the program works well for certain kinds of participants and not well for participants in other categories. This is useful information for both summative and formative evaluation, and it can be displayed in the form of a table that presents headcounts or mean scores of various groups or categories. Table 20 shows one form that such a table might take.

TABLE 18
Specific Objectives Mastered by
Varying Percentages of Program Students

Percent of students displaying mastery	Objective Numbers
76 - 100%	3, 11, 15, 16, 24, 25, 26, 33, 39, 42, 47
51 - 75%	4, 12, 14, 17, 18, 19, 22, 27, 30, 36, 43, 46
26 - 50%	1, 2, 6, 7, 20, 23, 28, 29, 34, 37, 38, 44, 45
0 - 25%	5, 8, 9, 10, 13, 21, 31, 32, 35, 40, 41

TABLE 19
Number of Students Showing Different Levels of
Test Performance on Seven Objectives (n = 135)

Objective	Level of Performance			Satisfied?
	Low	Middle	High	
#1	23	20	92	YES
#2	0	15	120	YES
#3	95	25	15	NO
#4	29	31	75	NO
#5	56	27	52	NO
#6	37	12	86	NO
#7	0	125	10	NO

Factor 1 might be "textbook used" in a program in which teachers selected one of four alternative textbooks. The "level" in this case would simply refer to the choice of textbook. If there were no Factor 2, the table would consist of just one row of mean achievement scores for students in groups using different textbooks. If, say, linguistic background of students was of interest, however, the three categories of Factor 2 might be Oriental, European, and Other. The table would then display the variation in achievement among different language groups with different textbooks in this program. A factor, of course, may have

TABLE 20
Format for a Table Classifying Students or Groups
According to Two Characteristics or "Factors"

Factor 1

		Level 1	Level 2	Level 3	Level 4
	Level 1				
Factor 2	Level 2				
	Level 3				

any number of levels, and its division into levels should be based upon the presumed significance of each to the program.

You might use *level of performance* on an achievement test as one factor defining cells in Table 20. These levels could be low, middle, and high scores, for example, or scores above and below the median. First, establish the range of scores to be classified within each level. Then enter in the table the number of students whose scores fall within each level. *Low* might be a score less than 30, *Middle*, a score from 30-50, and *High*, a score above 50. In order to show a relationship, a second factor is required, such as the number of years that the student's family has lived in the district if this is of interest. The table will show whether the second factor appears to be related to how well students performed on the measure used. You can determine whether the relationship observed is likely to be due to chance by performing a test of statistical significance. Which statistical test is appropriate with such tables varies according to the kind of data they present. You should consult a basic statistics text to select the right statistical test.

When you want to measure the degree of relationship between two quantifiable factors such as scores, number of days in attendance, or number of objectives passed, you can also calculate a correlation coefficient. Table 8 in Chapter 5 shows the basic format for setting up data to begin calculating a correlation between two measures. The first column lists the *names of people*—students or other participants. The X column might record the person's achievement score, and the Y column could show the number of years of formal schooling received by each person's mother. The correlation coefficient will then tell you to what extent students with better-educated mothers performed better on the achievement test. Your choice from among the many correlation coefficients you could calculate will be determined by the type of numbers that measures X and Y have produced. You should consult a statistics text to locate the correct correlation coefficient (see Fitz-Gibbon and Morris, 1987a).

Notes

1. Basic texts containing additional information on data processing are available. One such book is Feingold's *Introduction to Data Processing* (1975). If you will be using the *Statistical Package for the Social Sciences* (SPSS), you might consult Fitz-Gibbon and Morris (1987a).

2. Step-by-step procedures for standard setting can be found in Livingston and Zicky (1982).

3. See Fitz-Gibbon and Morris (1987a). A description of the use of a true and non-equivalent control group designs can be found in Fitz-Gibbon and Morris (1987b).

4. Sometimes the urge to report norm scores, when they are available, will overwhelm this chapter's admonition to graph only raw scores. Norm scores, after all, are easy to interpret. In these instances, consider this advice: Norm scores more accurately reflect raw scores among students who are scoring in the middle range—around the 50th percentile, the 5th stanine, or with z-scores between -1 and $+1$. Inaccuracy is less likely when you are dealing with average performance. But why chance it? Maybe the best thing to do is report the raw scores too, compare the graphs, and educate everyone concerned!

5. Advice on examining, reporting, and discussing time series designs is contained in Fitz-Gibbon and Morris (1987b, chap. 5); see also Campbell and Stanley (1966).

For Further Reading

Angoff, W.H. Scales, norms and equivalent scores. In R.L. Thorndike (Ed.), *Educational measurement*. Washington, D.C.: American Council on Education, 1971, 509-600.

Frechtling, J.A., & Myerberg, N.J. *Reporting test scores to different audiences*. ERIC/TM, Report 85. Princeton, NJ: Educational Testing Service.

Gronlund, N.E. Interpreting test scores and norms. In *Measurement and evaluation in teaching*. New York: Macmillan, 1976, 387-424.

References

Bloom, B. S. et al. (1956). *Taxonomy of educational objectives: The classification of educational goals. Handbook 1: Cognitive domain.* New York: Longman.

Campbell, D. A., & Fiske, D. W. (1959). Validation by the multitrait multimethod matrix. *Psychological Bulletin, 56,* 81-105.

Campbell, D. T., & Stanley, J. C. (1966). *Experimental and quasi-experimental designs for research.* Chicago: Rand McNally.

Cohen, J. (1960). A coefficient of agreement for nominal scales. *Educational and Psychological Measurement, 20,* 37-46.

Dotseth, M., Hunter, R., & Walker, C. B. (1978). Survey of test selectors' conerns and the test selection process. *CSE Report No. 107.* Los Angeles: Center for the Study of Evaluation, UCLA Graduate School of Education.

Feingold, (1975). *Introduction to data processing.* Dubuque, IA: Wm. C. Brown.

Fitz-Gibbon, C. T., & Morris, L. L. (1987a). *How to analyze data.* Newbury Park, CA: Sage.

Fitz-Gibbon, C. T., & Morris, L. L. (1987b). *How to design a program evaluation* (2nd ed.). Newbury Park, CA: Sage.

Fitz-Gibbon, C. T., & Morris, L. L. (1978). *How to calculate statistics.* Newbury Park, CA: Sage.

Fleiss, J. L. (1973). *Statistical methods for rates and proportions.* New York: John Wiley.

Glaser, R. (1963). Instructional technology and the measurement of learning outcomes. *American Psychologist, 18,* 510-522.

Guttman, L. (1970). Integration of test design and analysis. In *Proceedings of the 1969 Invitational Conference on Testing Problems* (pp. 53-65). Princeton, NJ: Educational Testing Service.

Hambleton, R. K., Swaminathan, H., Algina, J., & Coulson, D. B. (1978). Criterion-referenced testing and measurement: A review of technical issues and developments. *Review of Educational Research, 48*(1), 1-47.

Huynh, H. (1977). Two simple classes of mastery scores based on the beta-binomial model. *Psychometrika, 42,* 601-608.

Livingston, S. A., & Zicky, M. J. (1982). *Passing scores: A manual for setting standards of performance on educational and occupational tests.* Princeton, NJ: Educational Testing Service.

Morris, L. L., & Fitz-Gibbon, C. T. (1978). *How to deal with goals and objectives.* Newbury Park, CA: Sage.

Popham, W. J. (1978). *Criterion-referenced measurement.* Englewood Cliffs, NJ: Prentice-Hall.

Pyrczak, F. (1975-1976). A note on measures of the passage-dependence of reading test items. *Reading Research Quarterly, 11*(1), 112-117.

Swaminathan, H., Hambleton, R. K., & Algina, J. (1974). Reliability of criterion-referenced tests: A decision-theoretic formulation. *Journal of Educational Measurement, 11,* 263-267.

Appendix A:
A Table for Program-Test
Comparison (TPTC)

Test _____   Subject area _____

Type: □CRT □NRT □Unclear   Test level _____

Participant level _____

1 Test item	2 Objectives that match item	3 Importance of objective					4 Item content and format analysis		
		1	2	3	4	5	0	1	2

Rated by_____

Date_____

| box A | Total # of program objectives used for selection |

5 Item appropriateness for participants			6 Product of columns 3, 4, and 5	7
0	1	2		Summary figures

1 Test item	2 Objectives that match item	3 Importance of objective					4 Item content and format analysis		
		1	2	3	4	5	0	1	2

5 Item appropriateness for participants			6 Product of columns 3, 4, and 5	7
0	1	2		Summary figures

1 Test item	2 Objectives that match item	3 Importance of objective					4 Item content and format analysis		
		1	2	3	4	5	0	1	2

box B

Total # of items on the test

box C

of *different* objectives listed

5 Item appropriateness for participants			6 Product of columns 3, 4, and 5	7
0	1	2		Summary figures
				Grand Average
				Grand Tally (box D) ÷ total # of items on the test (box B) =
				Index of Coverage
				# of objectives listed in column 2 (box C) ÷ total # of program objectives (box A) =
				Index of Relevance
				# of products in column 6 (box E) ÷ total # of items on the test (box B) =

box D   Grand Tally

box E   # of products in column 6 > 0

Appendix B:
A Reminder of Some Common
Item Construction Errors

You might ask these questions in order to suggest ways of improving your own tests—or for evaluating the quality of the items on the tests you are considering for selection.

Questions Concerning All Test Items

- Do the items contain content or language that could be considered racially, ethnically, religiously, sexually, geographically, or economically biased?

Questions Concerning Essay Items

- Could it be that the question requiring an essay response would be more easily answered and scored through another type of item?
- Is the question ambiguous? That is, does it fail to clearly and accurately explain the depth and extent of the answer that is desired? For instance, does it neglect to mention how many reasons, examples, arguments, and the like are expected in order for the answer to receive full credit? Does it explain what it means by "describe," "outline," "state," or "compare"? Does it neglect to accurately explain what type of answer will receive full credit?
- Is the question too broad to be covered adequately in the time allotted?
- Are there clear criteria for scoring?

Questions Concerning Writing Prompts

- Is the topic one that some respondents may not have sufficient background experience and information to respond to?

Authors' Note: Many of the questions in this appendix were suggested by a document distributed by the New York State Education Department, Albany, titled *Improving the Classroom Test* (1968).

- Does the topic provide some respondents with an unfair opportunity to display their writing skills?

Questions Concerning Short Answer Items

- Is the statement to be completed too ambiguous to limit the correct answer to one or two specific words or phrases?
- Does the statement leave ambiguous the type of answer called for? The sentence "was found in ___" could be answered, for instance, by either a date or a location.
- Do short answer statements give unintended clues to the correct response by leaving blanks of differing lengths, or by indicating the number of letters of words to be filled in by broken lines?
- Does the omitted part of each question come in the middle or at the beginning of statements rather than at the end, where it belongs?
- Do items contain extraneous clues from grammatical structure, length of blank space, use of the article "a" or "an"?
- Could the type of information required be better handled through another type of question?
- Do items that require computation fail to describe the sort of answer required? For instance, do they neglect to explain the form in which fractions and decimals will be accepted, or whether units such as square yards or meters per second must be included in the answer?

Questions Concerning Multiple Choice Items

- Is a multiple choice format inappropriate to the outcome being measured?
- Is the language of the item complex or unclear, perhaps containing unfamiliar vocabulary?
- Do items have more than one correct answer?
- Do items have several central issues rather than a single one?
- Do responses or choices come at the beginning or the middle of the stem rather than at the end, where they belong?
- Are response alternatives grammatically inconsistent with *the stem*?
- Are response alternatives inconsistent with *one another*?
- Are some response alternatives implausible or easily eliminated by students who lack the information tested by the item?[1]
- Are the response alternatives arranged in an illogical or confusing order?
- Are the response alternatives interdependent or logically overlapping?
- Do the response alternatives include extraneous clues due to grammatical inconsistencies or length of response? Are the correct answers, for instance, generally longer than the incorrect ones?
- Is the *none of these* option used inappropriately?

- Across items, is the correct answer among alternatives likely to be found in the same position much of the time? For instance, is the correct alternative nearly always in the middle position?

Questions Concerning True-False Items

- Are items indefinite or ambiguous in meaning?
- Is the true-false format inappropriate for measuring this particular outcome?
- Are the items based on statements that have exceptions and qualifications that prevent them from being clearly true or false?
- Are the items based on opinion rather than fact?
- Is the central point of each question obscured by qualifications or difficult wording?
- Do the items contain statements that are partly true and partly false?
- Do items contain trick questions?
- Do items contain negative statements that are not properly highlighted?
- Do the items contain giveaway determiners such as *always* and *never*?
- If examinees will be required to correct the error in a true-false item, does the item fail to indicate which portions should be corrected?

Questions Concerning Matching Items

- Do the premises and responses contain heterogeneous lists combining diverse types of responses, rather than homogeneous lists as they should?
- Are the lists of premises and responses too long?
- Are the matching lists arranged inconveniently? For instance, are responses long and complex rather than just a few words?
- Are directions ambiguous about the basis upon which lists are to be matched? Do the directions fail to mention, for instance, whether a single premise can be matched with more than one response?
- Do the matching lists contain extraneous clues due to, for instance, grammatical construction, or verbal associations?
- Is the list of responses the same length as the list of premises so that students can gain points through the process of elimination?

Questions Concerning Observation and Rating Scales

- Is the observation or other subject of scrutiny likely to elicit a representative sample of the skill or behavior of interest?
- Is the content for the observation or rating clearly specified and standardized as appropriate? Are there clear task directions to those who are to be observed and indication of what materials, if any, they are to be provided? Are there clear specifications to sampling whatever is to be rated or observed?

- Are there clear directions and clear criteria for making ratings or for otherwise recording observations? Is it likely that two independent judges would agree on the rating to be given—or are personal biases likely to exert significant influence?
- Is it feasible to rate or observe the number of characteristics/elements that are planned, or is a rater likely to be overwhelmed and rendered ineffectual?
- Is there sufficient training and practice for raters to help ensure their reliability?

Note

1. Pay particular attention to this problem when looking at reading tests that present a short passage and then require students to answer a set of multiple choice questions about what they have read. Researchers have shown that many students can score better than chance on these items without reading the passage! A thorough discussion of this item characteristics can be found in Pyrczak (1975-1976).

Index

NOTES

NOTES

NOTES

NOTES